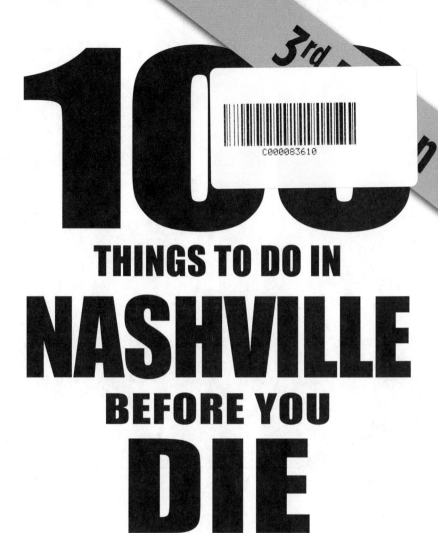

100

THINGS TO DO IN

NASHVILLE

BEFORE YOU

DIE

3rd

C000083610

I BELIEVE IN
NASHVILLE

© 2012 #ibelieveinnashville

3rd Edition

100

THINGS TO DO IN

NASHVILLE

BEFORE YOU

DIE

Enjoy exploring Nashville!
— Tom Adkinson

• •

TOM ADKINSON

REEDY PRESS

Library of Congress Control Number: 2022949243

ISBN: 9781681064222

Design by Jill Halpin

All photos are by the author unless otherwise noted.

Printed in the United States of America
23 24 25 26 27   5 4 3 2 1

DEDICATION

For Mike Alley, who helped me learn how to explore and enjoy both Nashville and life. I wish he were here to continue exploring and enjoying.

For the many people who continue to expand my horizons, both in Nashville and beyond.

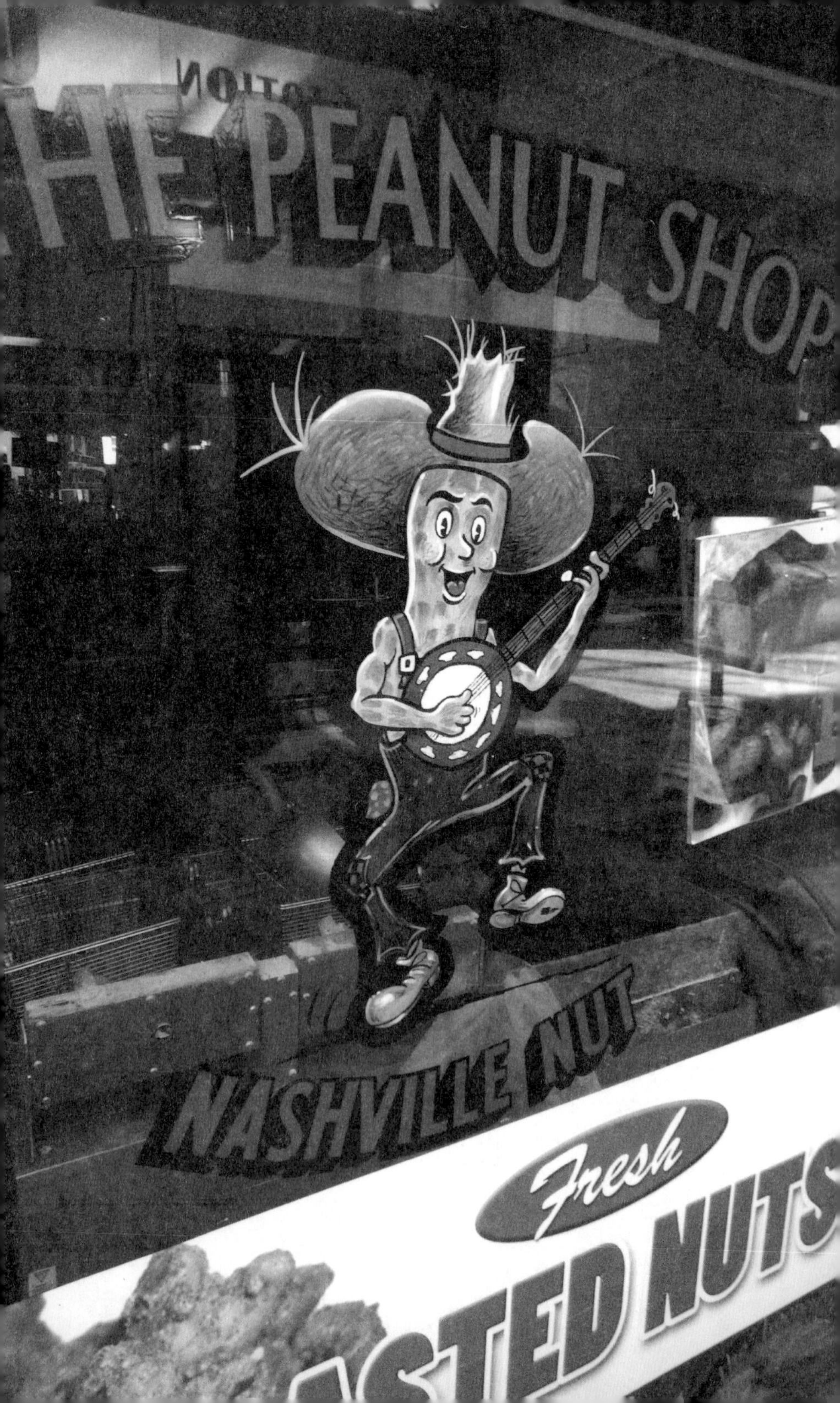
HE PEANUT SHOP
NASHVILLE NUT
Fresh
ASTED NUTS

CONTENTS

• •

Music and Entertainment

• •

Sports and Recreation

• •

Culture and History

• •

Shopping and Fashion

• •

PREFACE

Nashville is a happy place. I'm glad I grew up here and that I worked for many years in the city's tourism and hospitality industry. In a sense, I've been an ambassador for Nashville for decades, and writing this book is an extension of that volunteer job.

My family moved to Nashville in the late 1950s. Nashville certainly wasn't sleepy—it was the state capital, after all, and the Grand Ole Opry had brought it significant fame—but the population was only about 250,000. That number grew gradually, reaching 1 million in 2011, and now it is more than 1.3 million.

Much changed along the way, and to everyone's good fortune, much stayed the same. I find it amazing to identify aspects of Nashville that are unique (using that word precisely). No other city has the longest-running radio show in the world (the Opry). No other city has an exact replica of the Athenian Parthenon. No other city has the oldest professional theater for young audiences (the Nashville Children's Theatre). No other city has a festival devoted to the noble tomato that attracts upwards of 50,000 people on a hot August weekend to dress up in tomato costumes and indulge in other silly tomato behavior.

Nashville is rich in many kinds of music (the Country Music Hall of Fame is mere blocks from the National Museum of African American Music), history, sports, food (Goo Goo Clusters, hot chicken, meat and three restaurants, excellent barbecue), and

• •

even outdoor activities (you can take a veritable wilderness hike barely eight miles from the state capitol building).

Along with the music and frivolity, there are hard lessons to be learned here. Consider how the Union Army built a massive fort with formerly enslaved men, most of whom it didn't pay; how the 19th Amendment to the US Constitution, which secured women's right to vote, came within one legislative vote of failing; and how peaceful college students showed courage and strength fighting to end segregation.

Come explore Nashville with me. I offer 100 distinctive ways—and you probably could show me a few more.

FOOD
AND DRINK

PRESS "R"
FOR ROOFTOP

Downtown rooftops in old Nashville were places for pigeons and air-conditioning chillers, but architects changed their tune when fancy hotels started popping up like mushrooms after a summer rain. Yes, some Lower Broadway honky-tonks have rooftop bars, but hanging out with the hollering music fans there doesn't compare with being on top of the world at a spiffy hotel while enjoying a nice cocktail and a sunset view. Here are five to get you started: The Westin Hotel's L27 rooftop bar features a westward-facing infinity pool, while a 1956 Scenicruiser bus somehow got hoisted to Bobby's Rooftop Lounge at the Bobby Hotel. PROOF, atop the W Hotel, offers 270-degree views of the city, and lou/na (named for the Louisville & Nashville Railroad) in the Grand Hyatt perches on the 25th floor. There's even a rooftop bar with a Dolly Parton theme called White Limozeen at the Graduate Nashville Hotel, but Dolly herself isn't involved.

ROOFTOP BARS

L27
807 Clark Pl., 629-800-5070
L27nashville.com

Bobby's Rooftop Lounge
230 4th Ave. N, 615-782-7100
bobbyhotel.com

PROOF
300 12th Ave. S, 629-247-1282
proofnashville.com

lou/na
1000 Broadway, 615-622-4063
lounanashville.com

White Limozeen
101 20th Ave. N, 615-551-2700
graduatehotels.com/nashville/restaurant/white-limozeen

CHOW DOWN
AT A MEAT AND THREE

Disregard Nashville's fancy restaurants. The ones tied to Nashville's history and Nashvillians' hearts are unpretentious meat and threes. The silverware may not match, beverages usually come in plastic tumblers, and vinegar and hot sauce are standard table condiments. The category name tells it all. You've come for a meat and three vegetables. If you're smart, add dessert. Service often is along a steam line, where you'll choose from probably half a dozen meats and a dozen vegetables. Fried chicken, baked chicken, baked ham, beef tips, catfish, meatloaf, pork chops. Green beans, collard greens, cream corn, sweet potato casserole, mashed potatoes, fried okra, boiled okra, stewed tomatoes, macaroni and cheese. (Yes, macaroni and cheese is a vegetable!) Expect good cornbread. Some food historians say meat and threes originated in Nashville. All are very democratic. You may be sitting next to a banker, a day laborer, an office worker, a freelance writer, or a country music star. Everyone's the same at a good meat and three—hungry. Check out these long-time local favorites.

PLACES TO TRY MEAT AND THREES

City Cafe East
1455 Lebanon Pike, 615-742-8900
citycafeeast.com

Swett's Restaurant
2725 Clifton Ave., 615-329-4418
swettsrestaurant.com

Silver Sands Café
937 Locklayer St., 615-780-9900
silversandsnashville.com

Wendell Smith's
407 53rd Ave. N, 615-383-7114
wendellsmithsrestaurant.net

BUTTER A BISCUIT
AT THE LOVELESS CAFE

Biscuits are one Southern food that can prompt fierce debate, but nobody will turn down a plate of fresh-from-the-oven pillowy gems at the Loveless Cafe. Generations of Nashvillians have made what seemed to be a long trip out Highway 100 for a down-home meal at the Loveless. Biscuits and preserves were key. Today, the Loveless is at the northern terminus of the Natchez Trace Parkway and not far from I-40, so it seems easier to reach than when it was an outpost on the pre-interstate highway between Nashville and Memphis. Lon and Annie Loveless began selling fried chicken and biscuits here in 1951. Cafe ownership changed over the decades, but not the biscuits (up to 10,000 are baked daily) or the dedication to country cooking, homemade preserves, and delicious smoked meats. Expect competition for the cafe's 129 seats.

8400 Hwy. 100, 615-646-9700
lovelesscafe.com

TIP

In the heart of downtown, the biscuits at Kitchen Notes in the Omni Nashville Hotel have devoted fans. They are decidedly different from those at the Loveless, denser and more compact, and some are flavored up with cheddar cheese or chocolate chips.

omnihotels.com/hotels/nashville/dining/kitchen-notes

FREEZE YOUR BRAIN
AT BOBBIE'S DAIRY DIP

Bobbie's Dairy Dip is a brain-freezing, seven-decade trip back to the era of mom-and-pop ice cream and burger stands. Bobbie's started serving milkshakes, banana splits, burgers, and fresh-cut fries in 1951. The burgers aren't cooked until you order them, and about the only thing that has changed are a few menu updates (guacamole burgers and sweet potato fries, for instance) and some terribly creative milkshake names. Consider the Elmer Fuddge (a triple whammy with chocolate ice cream, chocolate syrup, and hot fudge) or the Chubby Checker (twist ice cream, hot fudge, peanut butter, and whipped cream). If you're deep enough into trivia, you'll understand why the Joey Dee milkshake recipe calls for peppermint. Order at one window; pick up at another. All seating is outdoors at well-worn picnic tables.

5301 Charlotte Ave., 615-463-8088
facebook.com/bobbiesdairydipcharlotteave

DO A GOOD DEED: DINE AT THE CAFÉ
AT THISTLE FARMS

You can feed your tummy and your soul at the Café at Thistle Farms. You should expect good food at an establishment this popular, and the soul-satisfying element comes from knowing that your patronage is helping a good cause. The café supports a nonprofit that heals, empowers, and employs women who have survived trafficking, prostitution, and addiction. The café is warm, friendly, open, and airy. It exudes hope and light. Perch at a counter to watch the traffic zip by on Charlotte Pike, fill a table in the main space, settle in for a spell on a comfy couch, or enjoy the quiet of the shaded back porch. Breakfast might be a simple croissant or a farmhouse breakfast bowl (local farm eggs, home fries with peppers and spinach, bright red tomatoes, and spicy ketchup). Lunch favorites include a spinach and berries salad topped with a scoop of chicken salad, and a brie and basil grilled cheese sandwich. After your meal, slide over to the retail space for Thistle Farms' highly popular natural body products (soaps, lotions, fragrances, and such).

5122 Charlotte Ave., 615-953-6440
thecafeatthistlefarms.org

DINE IN OR CARRY OUT
AT THE NASHVILLE FARMERS' MARKET

The Nashville Farmers' Market is a downtown institution that combines Tennessee's agricultural heritage with modern tourism. It is within sight of the capitol building. Whatever is fresh and right off the farm is in the Farm Sheds, where more than 150 farmers and producers offer colorful fruit, crisp vegetables, honey, jams, jellies, baked goods, and beautiful cuts of meat. The sheds are adjacent to the Market House, where several food court restaurants show Nashville's international flair—Mexican, Indian, Cajun, Asian, Caribbean, and more. Shops such as HeArt of Nashville showcase a variety of local art, craft, and gift choices. Check the calendar for seasonal events such as April's Strawberry Jubilee, June's Peach Jam, and November's Turnip Green Festival.

900 Rosa Parks Blvd., 615-880-2001
nashvillefarmersmarket.org

PLAY
VIETNAMESE PING PONG

One strip mall, two Vietnamese restaurants. Do you see a challenge here? That's the case in the 5800 block of Charlotte Pike, where you can bounce back and forth between competing restaurants Kien Giang (named for a province in Vietnam) and Miss Saigon. Neither place will break the bank as you compare the pho, various bahn mi (Vietnamese sandwiches on pillow-soft bread), spicy bo tai chanh (rare sliced beef in lime juice sauce), spring rolls, and vermicelli bowls laden with chicken, shrimp, beef, pork, or Vietnamese sausage. Miss Saigon's desserts include a green tea cheesecake.

Kien Giang
5825 Charlotte Pike, 615-353-1250
kiengiangtn.com

Miss Saigon
5849 Charlotte Pike, 615-354-1351
misssaigontn.com

TIP
With three area locations, the very casual Vui's Kitchen continues to introduce more people to Vietnamese cuisine. The original is in Berry Hill. vuiskitchen.com

BATTLE
OVER BARBECUE

The aroma of a barbecue pit can make you pull a U-turn in Nashville. If the police question your driving, just explain that the barbecue made you do it and ask whether you're headed in the right direction. The officer might even engage you in conversation about the best in town. Here are four places likely to be discussed (listed alphabetically to avoid argument).

STOP IN FOR SOME BARBECUE

Edley's Bar-B-Que
Edley's first pit was in the 12South neighborhood, but it has expanded to two other Nashville locations, one in Chattanooga and one (gasp) in southern Illinois. The menu is big, but one sandwich gets a lot of attention—the Tuck Special (smoked brisket, an over-easy egg, red and white barbecue sauce, pickles, and— get this—spicy pimento cheese).
Multiple locations
edleysbbq.com

Jack's Bar-B-Que
Jack Cawthon, seldom seen without his riverboat gambler hat, was smoking pork and brisket on Lower Broadway before Lower Broadway was cool. He's still there, and in two other locations. His place on West Trinity Lane is a classic family barbecue destination.
Three locations
jacksbarbque.com

Martin's Bar-B-Que Joint
Martin's started in rural/suburban Nolensville and then began opening in other area locations, plus Alabama, Kentucky, and South Carolina. Downtown visitors are closest to the one near the fancy Omni Hotel Nashville. Martin's brags on its whole-hog technique— and its coconut cake, pecan pie, and fudge pie.
Multiple locations
martinsbbqjoint.com

Peg Leg Porker
Pitmaster Carey Bringle, namesake of the Peg Leg Porker brand because of a losing battle with bone cancer, is one of the great personalities of the competitive barbecue world. He's even cooked at the James Beard House in New York. His one and only restaurant is at the edge of the Gulch. His merchandise includes a "Limpin' Ain't Easy" T-shirt.
903 Greaves St., 615-829-6023
peglegporker.com

JOIN
THE BURGER DEBATE

You can't win the "where's the best burger in town" debate, but you can hold your own with these nominees (listed alphabetically to avoid argument).

PLACES FOR GREAT BURGERS

Brown's Diner
Brown's really is *Cheers* and has the oldest beer permit in Nashville to prove it—along with legendary cheeseburgers, chili made daily, and Frito pie. The old portion, which defies gravity, is a streetcar and site of a well-worn 14-seat bar. Cold Bud and proximity to Music Row mean conversations are delicious, too. You might be having a burger while seated next to a star.
2102 Blair Blvd., 615-269-5509
thebrownsdiner.com

Dino's Restaurant
Even the owner doesn't understand how *Bon Appetit* picked Dino's for one of the three best burgers in America. Face it, Dino's is an East Nashville dive bar known best to the (very) late-night crowd. It doesn't even open until 4 p.m. except on weekends, when it serves a killer breakfast starting at noon. Follow in Anthony Bourdain's footsteps and check out this East Nashville classic.
411 Gallatin Pike, 615-226-3566
dinosnashville.com

Gabby's Burgers and Fries
It opened during the Great Recession and was an immediate hit. Burgers made with grass-fed beef and named for the owner's kids, an atmosphere that channels *Cheers* but without the beer, sweet potato fries, and thick shakes are the winning combo here. A message on the website sets the lighthearted tone: "Police, fire and military get 20% off. But not politicians! Just saying."
493 Humphreys St., 615-773-3119
gabbysburgersandfries.com

Pharmacy Burger Parlor & Beer Garden
This neighborhood hit claims recognition as Nashville's first biergarten and enjoys calling itself Nashville's "Wurst-Burger" joint because the staff not only makes memorable burgers, but it also grinds, stuffs, and smokes every sausage on the menu. Add phosphates, milkshakes, and ice cream sodas, and you'll see why the Pharmacy makes most people's lists.
731 McFerrin Ave., 615-712-9517
thepharmacyburger.com

DO A SLOW BURN
WITH NASHVILLE HOT CHICKEN

Until recent decades, few outside of Nashville's Black neighborhoods even knew about hot chicken. The legend, which has more than a hint of truth to it, dates to the 1930s. Thornton Prince's steady girl was more than suspicious of his wandering ways, so she sought retribution by doctoring up his favorite fried chicken enough to set him on fire. Instead of gasping for air, he asked for more. What became of the steady girl isn't documented, but Prince perfected the recipe and opened Prince's Hot Chicken Shack. Decades later, a few white customers latched on to Prince's not-really-secret dish. Other hot chicken restaurants have emerged, but all of them point back to Thornton Prince and his spiteful steady girl. Prince's itself is even uptown now, with a location in the Assembly Food Hall in the heart of downtown. Wise counsel says to start with the mild and work your way up.

5814 Nolensville Pike S, 615-810-9388
5055 Broadway Pl., Stall #2268
princeshotchicken.com

TIP

The free-admission Music City Hot Chicken
Festival on July 4 at East Park will put your
taste buds to a serious test. Multiple vendors vie
for your attention. Proceeds benefit the Friends
of Shelby Park & Bottoms.

hot-chicken.com

BEND AN ELBOW
AT A NASHVILLE TAPROOM

Tennessee is known for its whiskey, but Nashville has developed a solid reputation for another amber liquid—beer. Here are four breweries and taprooms (listed alphabetically to avoid favoritism), each with significant local followings. Bottoms up!

TIP

Nashville's beer festival calendar is busy spring, summer, and fall. The annual season seems to begin with the East Nashville Beer Fest in April. eastnashvillebeerfest.com

---

BREWERIES AND TAPROOMS TO VISIT

Little Harpeth Brewing

It's easy to make a Little Harpeth beer your first upon arriving in
Nashville or your last as you depart. That's because the Little Harpeth
taproom is in Terminal B at BNA, Nashville International Airport.
Little Harpeth says its brews are in the tradition of German lagers and
consistent with pre-prohibition beers of Middle Tennessee.
BNA Airport
littleharpeth.com

Nashville Brewing Company

This history-laden brewery traces its heritage to 1859, and the owner
tells the history of Nashville breweries from the early 1800s through
the 1950s on a monthly tour that includes two pints of your choice
(reservations required). Its Nashville Amber Lager label features the
state capitol building, and its Nashville 1897 Pilsner label is an image
of the Parthenon from the year it was built.
2312 Clifton Ave.
nashvillebrewing.com

Tennessee Brew Works

This brewery opened in 2013 and has special ties to Tennessee
agriculture. In 2018, it introduced the state's first
all-Tennessee grain beers, and its State Park Blonde Ale
is the official beer of Tennessee State Parks. The taproom is pure
Music City, with an open-mic night on Mondays, a songwriter's round
on Tuesdays, and bluegrass music on Wednesdays.
809 Ewing Ave.
tnbrew.com

Yazoo Brewing Company

Yazoo started brewing in 2003 and has moved twice for more space.
Its brewery and vibrant taproom are now on a 6.5-acre campus
north of downtown. Its beer menu is varied, and nostalgia drives
many fans to its Gerst Amber Ale, which honors the Gerst Brewery,
Nashville's original beer maker from the 1800s that never recovered
from Prohibition.
900 River Bluff Dr.
yazoobrew.com

DRESS UP
LIKE A TOMATO

Is a tomato a fruit or a vegetable? Even the US Supreme Court has weighed in on this not-so-weighty question, but the answer doesn't matter one bit during the only-in-Nashville Tomato Art Festival every August. The motto of this wacky community event sums it up well: "A Uniter, Not a Divider—Bringing Together Fruits and Vegetables!" It began in 2004 to promote a gallery's art show and grew like a runaway vine. The two-day attendance tops 50,000 tomato-heads for the Tomato King and Queen Contest, the Tomato 5K Run, and the Tomato Parade. Of course, there's a bloody Mary contest. Create your best tomato costume, and maybe even make one for your dog.

Throughout the Five Points Neighborhood
1160 Woodland St., 615-266-2070
tomatoartfest.com

MEASURE THE MERINGUE
ON ELLISTON PLACE

The meringue atop an Elliston Place Soda Shop chocolate or coconut pie might not really be a mile high, but that's still an apt description. The meringue that veteran waitress Linda Melton (she's known as "the Pie Lady") applies to the soda shop's pies is a work of art and the stuff of legend. Nashville was afraid it was going to lose the venerable restaurant in 2019, but it was saved with a short (but not simple) move next door. Regardless of real estate woes, the Elliston Place Soda Shop serves a powerfully good breakfast, shifts into meat and three territory later in the day, and hangs on until evening for early dinners or meals to take home. It opened in 1939 and is Nashville's oldest restaurant in its original location if you discount moving one door down the street. As with its pies, it is famous for its milkshakes, which are made with Nashville's Purity ice cream. Just ask the many fathers who have raced across the street from Saint Thomas Midtown Hospital while their wives were in labor. Sometimes, only a real milkshake will do.

2105 Elliston Pl., 615-327-1090
ellistonplacesodashop.com

PASS THE PEAS, PLEASE,
AT MONELL'S

"Enter as strangers, leave as friends." That's the motto at Monell's in the Germantown neighborhood. Breakfast, lunch, or dinner at Monell's is like a family reunion because you sit at communal tables, visit with whoever is seated near you, and respond when someone asks you to pass the peas, please. (Always pass to the left.) It's in an old house (built in 1898) with well-worn floors and a homey atmosphere. Even with only 72 seats, it can serve 10,000 people a month, and no one goes away hungry. Conversation flows across the tables as the fried chicken, pot roast, pork chops, green beans, cheese grits, crowder peas, turnip greens, salads, and desserts move along. If a bowl or platter is emptied, a full one magically appears. It's open 365 days a year, and the schedule oddity is late Saturday night, when breakfast is served from midnight until 3 a.m.

1235 6th Ave. N, 615-248-4747
monellstn.com

TIP
A second location, Monell's at the Manor, is in a historic mansion near Nashville International Airport. Service is family-style here, too, and it is the setting for numerous weddings and private events.

MAKE YOUR OWN
FIVE POINTS FOOD TOUR

Five Points is both a confusing intersection and the name of a neighborhood that offers everything from an independent hardware store and a tattoo parlor to a recording studio. More importantly, it's overrun with places to eat and drink. If one place is too busy, just stroll to another. Choices range from fancy to silly. Consider these: Margo Café & Bar (French inspired, with Southern influences), the Treehouse (a family home transformed into a farm-to-table restaurant), 3 Crow Bar (for beer, bushwhackers, burgers, and fried green tomato BLTs), Noble's Beer Hall (for, well, beer, but barbecue, too), Boston Commons (an unexpected collision of Boston seafood and Southern accents), I Dream of Weenie (for inventive hot dogs served from a converted VW bus), and Five Points Pizza (a consistent winner in local pizza ratings).

Where Woodland St., Clearview Ave., and N 11th St. collide
visitmusiccity.com/visitors/neighborhoods/eastnashville

EAT SIMPLY
AT TENNESSEE'S OLDEST RESTAURANT

The motto says it all: "It's always chili weather at Varallo's." That's been the case since 1907, when Italian immigrant Frank Varallo, Sr. opened his first "chile parlor" in downtown Nashville. Other chili purveyors came and went, but Varallo's persevered and now is Tennessee's oldest restaurant. It's plain and simple. You can get a solid breakfast or a meat and three, but you really should get the chili. Most famous is "chili three ways." That means meaty chili, snipped-up pieces of spaghetti, and bits of tamales. The business stayed in the Varallo family until 2020, but the new owner acquired the Varallo recipes.

239 4th Ave. N, 615-256-1907
varallosrestaurants.com

VISIT
"NASHVILLE'S WINE COUNTRY"

The picturesque, even idyllic, expanse of Arrington Vineyards had humble beginnings in 2003 when the first vines were planted on a 25-acre former hog farm. Land from a cattle farm expanded the operation, and then came yet another farm with a barn and a farmhouse. The owners, including country singer Kix Brooks, began making award-winning wines and inviting guests to tastings and musical events. Bring your own picnic, listen to some music, taste some wine, and sample a "Frosé" (a frozen rosé wine drink). Arrington Vineyards is south of Nashville and a lot closer than Napa Valley.

6211 Patton Rd., Arrington, TN, 615-395-0102
arringtonvineyards.com

TIP
Arrington Vineyards is far from alone in Tennessee wine production. Statewide, there are 65 wineries and more than 80 vineyards. tennesseewines.com

---

DINE ELEGANTLY IN HISTORY
AT THE STANDARD

The Standard at the Smith House has something that has become rare in today's restaurants—standards. The Standard expects its guests to dress appropriately when visiting to enjoy its excellent food served in historic and elegant surroundings. Yes, there's a dress code. It's not coat-and-tie stiff, but it is specific—and that sets the tone for memorable dining experiences, not just meals. The Smith House was built in the late 1840s and is the only grand townhouse of that era remaining in downtown Nashville. The structure is much larger than it appears from the street, housing the public restaurant and lounge, a private club, and even a ballroom. It's the place for special occasions—or occasions you want to make special.

167 Rosa Parks Blvd., 615-254-1277
smithhousenashville.com

KEEP A TRADITION ALIVE
AT INTERNATIONAL MARKET

Nashvillians feared losing an important piece of culinary history when it became clear Belmont University's growth would obliterate the International Market, a landmark institution that had introduced the city to real Thai food in 1975. Owners Win and Patti Myint were more than restaurateurs. They were cultural ambassadors who helped Nashville develop a sense of international citizenship. Belmont University did supplant the restaurant with a spectacular performing arts center, but two of Win and Patti's children (Arnold and Anna) kept the restaurant's spirit alive by opening what they call International Market 2 directly across the street. Lunch offers a huge variety of items from a steam line, and menu service takes over at dinnertime. As Arnold told the *Nashville Scene* newspaper, "It's a tribute restaurant. But just like a tribute band, we're going to put in our own twist. We're gonna keep the words, but we gotta put our own funk in there, too."

2013 Belmont Blvd., 615-297-4453
im2nashville.com

MUSIC
AND ENTERTAINMENT

CLIMB TO
THE MOUNTAINTOP:
THE GRAND OLE OPRY

The Grand Ole Opry is the longest-running radio show in the world and almost certainly is the most famous. Go. There's no argument. Experiencing the peculiar spectacle of a live radio show (complete with commercials and square dancers) that is unscripted and never the same show twice truly is an only-in-Nashville treat. It went on the air in 1925 on then-tiny WSM-AM radio, which soon launched a 50,000-watt signal that reached most of the nation. It's now also online and in part on TV. Be part of the show at the Grand Ole Opry House (4,400 padded seats) in the suburbs or at the Ryman Auditorium (space for 2,300 rear ends on hardwood church pews) downtown. Optional tours of the backstage dressing room area add to the experience.

600 Opry Mills Dr., 615-871-OPRY
opry.com

GET IN TUNE
AT THE MUSICIANS HALL OF FAME

The Musicians Hall of Fame and Museum may be in Nashville, but it's not a Nashville museum. To explain: This major attraction salutes the work of the mostly anonymous studio musicians from all over the nation, not just Nashville. Its focus stretches to powerhouse recording centers such as Muscle Shoals, Memphis, Los Angeles, and Detroit and the music behind songs recorded by everyone from Dean Martin to Smokey Robinson and from Garth Brooks to the Carpenters. Guitarist Duane Eddy, one of few musicians with a public persona, narrates an excellent film in which he explains how super-talented musicians can turn "three minutes in a closed room into a lifetime of memories." A huge bonus here is the GRAMMY Museum Gallery, an interactive facility where you can perform onstage and interact with every aspect of the recording process. With the privacy of headphones, you can play electric drums, keyboard, bass, and guitar, or sing along with Ray Charles and the Raelettes. See for yourself the complex process of cutting a record.

401 Gay St., 615-244-3263
musicianshalloffame.com

VISIT
THE "SMITHSONIAN OF COUNTRY MUSIC"

There is a reservoir of peace and serenity just a block from the honky-tonk madness of Lower Broadway—the Country Music Hall of Fame and Museum. Like the honky-tonks, it's packed with music and energy, but the volume is turned way, way down. You don't have to know much about country music or even listen to it all that much to appreciate this top-notch museum. It has two million artifacts (not all visible at one time, of course) that tell the story of Nashville's special calling card to the world. There are vintage video clips, recorded sound, famous instruments, manuscripts, and even Elvis Presley's "Solid Gold Cadillac." Limited-engagement exhibitions complement the core exhibit, "Sing Me Back Home." No wonder it's called the "Smithsonian of country music." Plan on at least two or three hours, but realize your ticket is good all day. That means you can dive into a nearby honky-tonk for a cold beer and a tear-jerking song and return for more museum exploration.

222 Rep. John Lewis Way S, 615-416-2001
countrymusichalloffame.org

TIP

Buy the add-on ticket for Historic RCA Studio B on Music Row, where Eddy Arnold, Waylon Jennings, Dolly Parton, Jim Reeves, Willie Nelson, the Everly Brothers, Roy Orbison, and that fellow from Memphis named Elvis Presley all recorded. Studio B delivered 35,000 songs, 1,000 Top 10 hits, and 40 million-selling songs.

GET UNDER THE TENT
AT AMERICANAFEST

The music called Americana is a melting pot of influences. Under its huge tent are roots, folk, country, blues, soul-based music, and more—and a list of artists you'll hear on an Americana station is as diverse as Gretchen Peters, Jim Lauderdale, Sister Sadie, Taj Mahal, Keb' Mo', Sheryl Crow, Jason Isbell, Rhiannon Giddens, and the Milk Carton Kids. The September celebration called AMERICANAFEST can wear you to the nubs—six straight nights, more than 50 venues (tiny to great big) all over the city, and 700 live performances, plus seminars, panel discussions, and a giant awards show in the Ryman Auditorium. You can test your stamina with a weeklong pass or do some sampling. It's unlike any music festival you've ever attended.

Multiple venues, 615-386-6936
americanamusic.org

MAYBE GET ON TV
AT CMA FEST

The odds aren't good that your smiling face makes the final cut of the network TV special that comes out of every CMA Fest, but your chances are zero if you don't dive into one of the biggest musical events of the year. This early-June fixture on the Nashville entertainment calendar began modestly in 1972 as an Opry Trust Fund event that drew 5,000 people to the Municipal Auditorium. My, how it has grown. It now is a four-day, multi-venue festival, and total attendance can push 90,000. There are nightly concert production shows at Nissan Stadium (try to make yourself heard over the 50,000 others inside the football stadium with you), plus daytime concerts at Riverfront Park along the Cumberland River and (praise be!) some events in the air-conditioned Music City Center. The big gigs at CMA Fest are ticketed, of course, but there's a good amount of free-access entertainment with some surprisingly big-name artists, too. One of the free activities is scoring the quality of costumes that some of the most devoted country music fans wear to this big, sweaty party.

Nissan Stadium, Music City Center, other venues
cmafest.com

BE A
HONKY-TONK MAN (OR GAL)

Give into the urge to channel Johnny Horton or Dwight Yoakam (Horton wrote the classic "I'm a Honky Tonk Man," and he and Yoakam had hits with it decades apart) by exploring the mass of beer-serving, live-music-playing, no-longer-smoky honky-tonks on Lower Broadway. Some have great stories (Tootsie's Orchid Lounge was a hangout for Opry members when the Opry was across the alley at the Ryman Auditorium), and others sport A-list country music artists' names. Among anchor establishments in addition to Tootsie's (which has an outpost at Nashville's airport) are Legends Corner, the Second Fiddle, Layla's, the Stage, and Robert's Western World. It's impossible to beat a good band and a Recession Special at Robert's. That's a fried bologna sandwich with lettuce and tomato on Texas toast with chips, a mini-Moon Pie, and a cold Pabst Blue Ribbon Beer for $6, tax included. Remember to tip your server and the band.

Broadway between 2nd and 5th Avenues
visitmusiccity.com/visitors/honkytonkhighway

SWING LOW
WITH THE FISK JUBILEE SINGERS

One of Music City's greatest musical stories is the Fisk Jubilee Singers, the a capella ensemble that saved a struggling college created just after the Civil War to educate formerly enslaved people. The group formed in 1871 to tour and raise funds for Fisk University. Along the way, they introduced slave songs to the world (including to Queen Victoria in England in 1873) and preserved an American musical tradition. Initial results were rocky, but a fire had been lit. The Fisk Jubilee Singers went to the White House and on to Europe. America honored them in 2008 with the National Medal of Arts. Today's Fisk Jubilee Singers carry on a great tradition, so watch for a public performance. Grab a ticket if you see a booking, especially if it's at the acoustically marvelous Ryman Auditorium.

fiskjubileesingers.org

DREAM OF WRITING A SONG
AT THIS HALL OF FAME

Don't you wish you could write a song, have a star record it, and pluck royalty checks from your mailbox every month? Only a few people experience that, and Nashville salutes them, but in surprisingly modest fashion. The Nashville Songwriters Hall of Fame isn't a grand edifice. It's not even its own building. Still, you could spend hours here, reveling in songs you know by heart. Did you know Gene Autry wrote "Here Comes Santa Claus"? Can you guess why Chuck Berry is honored here? Did you know that John Prine once was a postal carrier? The Nashville Songwriters Hall of Fame is a modestly sized gallery of artifacts and electronics in a corner of the Music City Center, Nashville's gigantic convention center. Treasures include a handwritten letter from Hank Williams to his publisher doubting the quality of "I Saw the Light" and a first draft of Paul Craft's "Dropkick Me Jesus Through the Goalposts of Life." Push buttons to your heart's content, and keep listening. Admission is free.

201 Rep. John Lewis Way S, 615-460-6556
nashvillesongwritersfoundation.com

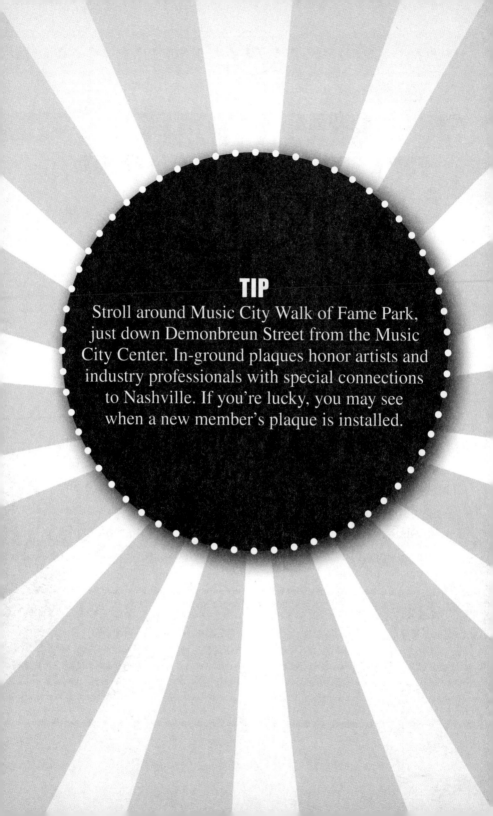

TIP

Stroll around Music City Walk of Fame Park, just down Demonbreun Street from the Music City Center. In-ground plaques honor artists and industry professionals with special connections to Nashville. If you're lucky, you may see when a new member's plaque is installed.

GRAB A TICKET
FOR A BRIDGESTONE ARENA EVENT

Arena shows are a huge part of the music industry, and one of many artists' favorite venues is the building that resembles a flying saucer crowned with a radio antenna at Sixth and Broadway adjacent to Nashville's honky-tonk pandemonium. It's the Bridgestone Arena, one of Nashville's biggest municipal investments at $144 million when it opened in 1996. (That seems modest now that Nashville is staring at $2 billion for a football stadium.) The Nashville Predators are its primary tenants, but go see an event other than a hockey game here. The facility regularly ranks as one of the nation's best arenas. Regardless of the event, you'll probably holler at the top of your lungs at some point, whether it's for Brad Paisley, Reba McEntire, U2, Michael Bublé, Smashing Pumpkins, a professional bull rider, a glittering figure skater, a gymnast who scores a perfect 10, or a basketball player who slams home a dunk to win a conference championship. Seating capacity is 20,000 for center-stage concerts.

501 Broadway, 615-770-7800
bridgestonearena.com

KEEP THE VIBE ALIVE
IN PRINTERS ALLEY

Before today's honky-tonk revelry mushroomed on Lower Broadway, another downtown entertainment district was famous—Printers Alley. It really is an alley, and it really has roots in printing and publishing from the 1800s. Its entertainment fame evolved in the 1940s, when Nashville's entertainers and musicians wanted places to play, and Nashville residents and visitors wanted places to eat and drink. Liquor by the drink wasn't legal until 1968, but club owners had workarounds for the booze, and entertainment always is in demand. Who performed? Try Etta James, Chet Atkins, Jerry Lee Lewis, Boots Randolph, Waylon Jennings, Andy Griffith, stripper Heaven Lee, and many more. Printers Alley waxed and waned over the decades, but it's going strong today. Establishments such as Skull's Rainbow Room, the Bourbon Street Blues and Boogie Bar, and the Fleet Street Pub keep the vibe alive.

Between 3rd and 4th Avenues North and Union and Commerce
nashvilledowntown.com/go/printers-alley

HEAR SONGWRITERS' MAGIC
AT TIN PAN SOUTH

Now into its fourth decade, the Tin Pan South Songwriters Festival every spring is the largest songwriters' festival in the world. For five days, you can bask in the genius of as many as 400 carefully selected songwriters in shows at up to 10 venues around the city (places such as the City Winery, the Station Inn, the Bluebird Cafe, the Country Music Hall of Fame and Museum, and 3rd and Lindsley). There are two shows per night at each venue. For less intense encounters with songwriters throughout the year, check out places such as the Commodore Grille, the Listening Room Cafe, and the Millennium Maxwell House Hotel.

Multiple venues, 615-256-3354
tinpansouth.com

TIP

Finding a songwriters' night—or any other kind of entertainment in Nashville—is easy. Let nowplayingnashville.com be your researcher. The nonprofit website is an initiative of the Community Foundation of Middle Tennessee.

BRING A CHAIR
OR A BLANKET
TO MUSICIANS CORNER

Throughout the year, people visit Centennial Park to marvel at Nashville's full-scale replica of the Parthenon, but in late spring and early autumn, music lovers gravitate to the southwest corner of the sprawling park for a concert series called Musicians Corner. Originators took inspiration from London's Hyde Park Speakers' Corner. The concerts are a gift to everyone from the Centennial Park Conservancy, the park's "friends" group. Concerts burst forth on Friday and Saturday evenings in May, June, and September, and also during a three-day celebration over Memorial Day weekend. More than 1,500 artists have performed since the series began in 2010. Among them are Vince Gill, Emmylou Harris, Chris Stapleton, the Blind Boys of Alabama, the Fairfield Four, Preservation Hall Jazz Band, Jars of Clay, St. Paul and the Broken Bones, the Secret Sisters, Elizabeth Cook, and Ruby Amanfu. Aside from the talent on stage, Musicians Corner has a particularly sterling attribute—admission is free. Bring your own chair or blanket.

Centennial Park, 615-862-6810
musicianscornernashville.com

JOURNEY TO THE BLUEGRASS MECCA
OF THE STATION INN

There's an island of bluegrass music in the sea of high-rise hotels, pricey condos, and fancy restaurants in the Gulch. It's the Station Inn, a 200-seat club in a nondescript, one-story building that was popular long before anyone even dreamed of tall buildings in this part of town. This is the place every bluegrass band wants to play—and the place bluegrass stars and legends perform. Bill Monroe, the Father of Bluegrass Music himself, sometimes would come over after appearing at the Grand Ole Opry, watch from the back of the house, and then stroll through the audience and ask whether he could play in. That's like having God ask whether he can come to a Wednesday night meeting with you. Parking is a challenge in the Gulch, but a night of some of the best bluegrass in the world is worth the effort.

402 12th Ave. S, 615-255-3307
stationinn.com

TIP

Feeling the need for a little faith after living it up too much? Check out "Sunday Gospel with Val Storey and Friends" at the Station Inn. It's an afternoon show, so you don't even have to get out of bed early. Pizza, beer, and probably some amazing grace are available.

GET IN THE GROOVE
AT THE NATIONAL MUSEUM
OF AFRICAN AMERICAN MUSIC

The National Museum of African American Music's CEO describes the museum's stature succinctly: "The museum puts an exclamation point on Nashville's brand as Music City." NMAAM (pronounced "nay-ma'am" by those in the know) tells the long and diverse story of Black music's impact on American culture, starting in the 17th century when enslaved Africans were first brought to North America. The central corridor is "Rivers of Rhythm," where a film examines 50 genres and subgenres of African American musical innovation, development, history, and achievement. From there, "Wade the Water" is about gospel, "Crossroads" examines the blues, "A Love Supreme" focuses on jazz, "One Nation Under a Groove" looks at R&B, and "The Message" delves into hip-hop. One very cool exhibit lets you perform in a choir led by Nashville gospel legend Bobby Jones. NMAAM is in the heart of Nashville, literally and figuratively, because it is next door to the historic Ryman Auditorium.

510 Broadway, 615-301-8724
nmaam.org

GET CINEMATIC
AT THE BELCOURT

Forget Netflix. Forget IMAX. Forget the multi-plex with Lord knows how many screens. Go see a movie for real at the Belcourt Theatre. The Belcourt, Nashville's nonprofit film center, is a two-screen gem (plus a 35-seat screening room for special uses) in Hillsboro Village that oozes history and nostalgia. It's where you go to relive memories with a classic such as *Casablanca* or *Citizen Kane* or to see an independent film that just got an Oscar nomination. The building itself is a Nashville treasure. It opened in 1925 with 800 seats for silent movies, was home to the Grand Ole Opry from 1934 to 1936, and survived the movie industry's myriad changes over the decades. It presents 300 films a year (2,300 screenings), and the array makes your head spin—just like the reels of the giant projector overhead. Everything got totally spiffed up in 2016 with a $5-million renovation. Programming takes some interesting turns. For instance, Mondays are for music films. This is Music City, you know.

2102 Belcourt Ave., 615-846-3150
belcourt.org

GET LOST
AT THE GAYLORD OPRYLAND RESORT

Employees at the 2,888-room Gaylord Opryland Hotel have joked that the American Heart Association should endorse the sprawling resort because of all the walking you'll do here. If you get lost, you won't be the first. All of those guestrooms, plus an incredible amount of convention space, gardens, and public areas, are under one roof—if you keep finding portals into the next dimension. The hotel was built over several years, and each addition adjoined what was previously built. The latest was a $90-million waterpark called Soundwaves. Needless to say, you can walk and walk and walk in air-conditioned comfort while logging more than your daily allotment of steps and pleasing your cardiologist. Three garden and fountain areas are particularly appealing. One covers almost five acres and has an actual river that was christened with samples of rivers from around the world. The hotel's well-traveled friends used miniature Jack Daniel's bottles to mail the water to Nashville. As you might expect, the hotel goes all-out with Christmas decorations and events.

2800 Opryland Dr., 615-889-1000
gaylordhotels.com

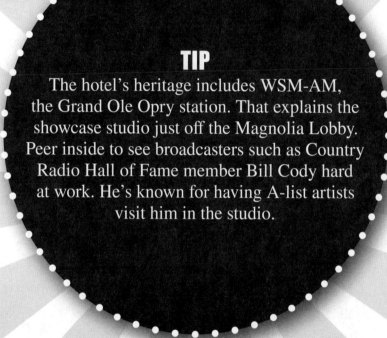

TIP

The hotel's heritage includes WSM-AM, the Grand Ole Opry station. That explains the showcase studio just off the Magnolia Lobby. Peer inside to see broadcasters such as Country Radio Hall of Fame member Bill Cody hard at work. He's known for having A-list artists visit him in the studio.

BRING YOUR GUITAR OR BANJO
TO A FULL MOON PICKIN' PARTY

You don't have to bring your own instrument to a Full Moon Pickin' Party at Percy Warner Park, but it's perfectly OK if you do. You won't end up on stage, but you very well may settle into a jam session with other partygoers. The Friday closest to the full moon from May through October brings out bluegrass pickers and bluegrass fans for a night of hot licks, musical camaraderie, and food. Three headline acts perform on the main stage, and impromptu jam sessions crop up wherever there's a cluster of people with their own guitars, banjos, dulcimers, bass fiddles, and other acoustic instruments. Bring your own picnic, or patronize a food truck. Admission is charged (the parties are fundraisers for Percy Warner Park and Edwin Warner Park), but your ticket includes water, soft drinks, and (this is true) up to three beers. Beer and bluegrass are natural companions.

TIP

This party concept is so good that the Friends of Shelby Park and Shelby Bottoms stage the Cornelia Fort Pickin' Party monthly from May through August. Go for local bands, craft beer, wine, and food vendors. Bring your own musical instrument for jam sessions and get an extra drink ticket. friendsofshelby.org/pickin-parties

---

KEEP AN EYE
ON THE TENNESSEE
PERFORMING ARTS CENTER

You'll want to watch for news about the Tennessee Performing Arts Center (TPAC)—not just for which productions are booked in this three-theater complex just across from the state capitol building, but because it may disappear, or at least somehow relocate. TPAC is where you go to see Broadway touring shows on a big stage and to enjoy concerts, comedy acts, lectures, and other events. TPAC is home to three resident artistic companies—Nashville Opera, Nashville Ballet, and Nashville Repertory Theatre—and its theaters range from 256 to 2,472 seats. So why might it disappear? TPAC is inside a state-owned building that is in a prime location for redevelopment, and there have been rumblings about the fate of the office tower that sits on top of the theater complex.

505 Deaderick St., 615-782-4040
tpac.org

SING JOHNNY CASH AND PATSY CLINE SONGS
IN YOUR HEAD AT THEIR MUSEUMS

One downtown address showcases two American music giants—
Johnny Cash and Patsy Cline. The Johnny Cash Museum and
the Patsy Cline Museum go beyond memorabilia collections.
They are vehicles taking you to yesteryear and entertaining you
today. When Cash handed 9-year-old Bill Miller a harmonica at
a concert, Miller began a half-century of collecting Cash-related
items. Artifacts honor Cash's music, plus his movie and TV work.
(Did you know he starred with Kirk Douglas in *A Gunfight*?)
The Patsy Cline Museum salutes a singer who broke ground for
women in country music. She made a splash on national TV
(*Arthur Godfrey's Talent Scouts*), is said to be the only person
bold enough to ask for Grand Ole Opry membership, scored
hit after hit on country and pop charts, and was the first female
country singer to headline in Las Vegas. A tragic airplane crash
ended her life, but the museum doesn't dwell on that. Instead, it
leaves you admiring the artistry that delivered a "Greatest Hits"
album that was on Billboard's charts for 722 weeks.

Johnny Cash Museum
119 3rd Ave. S, 615-256-1777
johnnycashmuseum.com

Patsy Cline Museum
119 3rd Ave. S, 615-454-4722
patsymuseum.com

TIP

Make it a celebrity museum trifecta by driving 75 miles west of Nashville to Loretta Lynn's Ranch in Hurricane Mills. In addition to being a museum to the Grand Ole Opry and Country Music Hall of Fame star, the ranch is a camping, RV, event, and concert destination.

931-296-7700
lorettalynnranch.net

DELIGHT IN THE TALENT
OF THE TIME JUMPERS

Just as Olympic swimmers like to play in the family pool or airline pilots like to fly tiny prop planes for personal enjoyment, Nashville's stellar professional musicians often play just for fun. That's the genesis of The Time Jumpers, 10 super musicians who come together at the 3rd and Lindsley club many Monday nights. Their jam sessions started in 1998 in a much smaller place (read about the Station Inn on page 44), but they soon had fans—and Grammy nominations—and needed more room. An evening with The Time Jumpers comes with a guarantee of extraordinary musicianship, great singing, wonderful camaraderie, and cold beer. Membership has changed, but only slightly, over the years. Today's Time Jumpers include "Ranger Doug" Green from Riders in the Sky, steel guitar virtuoso Paul Franklin, fiddlers Larry Franklin and Joe Spivey, and vocalist Wendy Moten, whom you probably recognize from NBC's *The Voice*.

818 3rd Ave. S, 615-259-9891
3rdandlindsley.com and thetimejumpers.com

REVERT TO CHILDHOOD
AT THE NASHVILLE CHILDREN'S THEATRE

Nashville is famous for its musical heritage (the Fisk Jubilee Singers date to 1871, and the Grand Ole Opry began in 1925), but it has a special claim to fame in the theatrical world, too. The Nashville Children's Theatre (NCT) is America's oldest professional theatre for young audiences. It all began in 1931, when the Junior League staged "Aladdin and His Wonderful Lamp." NCT's productions were in various locations for many years, including the Belcourt Theater (page 47), before settling into a multi-faceted home just seven blocks and a world away from Lower Broadway's honky-tonks. Its productions are aimed at various age levels, and it even has an incubator program called the Hatchery to develop new plays for young audiences. Treat your own kids, a grandchild, a favorite niece, or a neighbor family with youngsters to an NCT show—and don't forget your own ticket.

25 Middleton St., 615-252-4675 (box office)
nashvillechildrenstheatre.org

LAUGH UP A STORM
AT ZANIES

Nashville may be marinated in music, but its comedy scene is well regarded, too. Its central location in the US makes it appealing to always-on-the-road comics, especially because audiences are loyal to Zanies Comedy Club on 8th Avenue South. The club is relatively small (about 300 seats), and comics enjoy its vibe. Nashvillian Killer Beaz, who tours extensively, especially likes Zanies because he says he gets to go home after performing. Elsewhere, comedians who can pack larger houses especially like the Ryman Auditorium and even the Bridgestone Arena, and fans of improv target the Third Coast Comedy Club in Marathon Village.

2025 8th Ave. S, 615-269-0221
nashville.zanies.com

TIP

The Nashville Comedy Festival every April showcases more than 20 comedians in venues of all sizes and all over the city. nashcomedyfest.com

CAP OFF SUMMER
AT LIVE ON THE GREEN

Labor Day is the unofficial end of summer, and Nashville caps off the season in grand style with a music festival called Live on the Green. It's not just any ol' music festival—it's a free music festival that over the years has booked artists such as Sheryl Crow, Alabama Shakes, the Mavericks, Black Pumas, Steve Earle, Ben Folds, St. Paul & the Broken Bones, Ruby Amanfu, Guster, and Bre Kennedy. The setting is the two-acre Public Square Park, and the stage's backdrop is the Metro Courthouse. Lightning 100, one of the nation's top independent radio stations, presents the free shows for five nights. Expect three dozen or more artists. Bring a blanket or a folding chair, and enjoy music in the summertime.

3rd Ave. N and Union St., 615-242-5600
liveonthegreen.com

Courtesy of the Tennessee Titans

SPORTS
AND RECREATION

YELL "GOOOAAALLL"
AT GEODIS PARK

It was a trifecta for Nashville when Major League Soccer's Nashville SC joined the NFL's Tennessee Titans and the NHL's Nashville Predators in representing Music City in major league sports. The victory of simply joining the league grew bigger in 2022 when play began in 30,000-seat GEODIS Park, the largest soccer-specific stadium in the US and Canada. Watching a match in GEODIS Park is an up-close-and-personal experience because the last row of seats is only 150 feet from the touchline. It's definitely a major league event. GEODIS, by the way, is a French logistics company whose North American headquarters is only nine miles from the stadium.

501 Benton Ave., 615-750-8800
nashvillesc.com

ADMIRE THE CUMBERLAND RIVER
FROM ABOVE

It's very cool to walk across a Cumberland River bridge while the *General Jackson* showboat, a string of barges, or pleasure boats glide beneath you—especially when you don't have to worry about automobile traffic zipping behind you. You have two opportunities in Nashville. Cars and trucks rumbled across downtown's Seigenthaler Bridge from 1909 until 1998, when it morphed into one of the longest pedestrian bridges in the world (3,150 feet). A dividend here is a great view of Nashville's skyline. Upriver several miles is a much narrower but modern bridge built for pedestrians and bicyclists. It comes off a limestone bluff on the east side of the river and puts you at the tip of the Shelby Bottoms Natural Area and Shelby Park (1,200 acres of urban nature) on the west side. The bridge is a necessary link in a 13-mile greenway route from downtown to Percy Priest Dam. Bike the Greenway offers rental bicycles nearby.

nashvilledowntown.com/go/shelby-street-pedestrian-bridge

615-862-8400
greenwaysfornashville.org

615-920-1388
bikethegreenway.net

EXPERIENCE BASEBALL HISTORY
WITH THE NASHVILLE SOUNDS

When the 10,000-seat First Horizon Park opened in 2015, Nashville baseball took a trip back into history because the modern downtown stadium is on the site of the historic Sulphur Dell, where baseball was played from 1870 to 1963. Before the AAA Nashville Sounds team relocated from an aging stadium just a few miles away, fans worried a city icon might disappear. Never fear, because First Horizon Park's guitar-shaped scoreboard is integral to the stadium's identity. Keeping with Nashville's entertainment tradition, the scoreboard sports a 4,200-square-foot LED video screen. Numerous neighborhood bars and restaurants are within walking distance for pre- and post-game festivities.

19 Junior Gilliam Way, 615-690-4487
nashvillesounds.com

TIP

Every June, check for the City of Hope Celebrity Softball Game at First Horizon Park during CMA Fest. The game pits country music stars against each other, some of whom are very serious about winning and some of whom are happy to earn participation ribbons.

CHEER
FOR THE MIGHTY TITANS

Fans wearing the two-tone blue jerseys of the Tennessee Titans are out in force in Nashville when football season rolls around. The NFL Titans are in the American Football Conference South along with the Houston Texans, Indianapolis Colts, and Jacksonville Jaguars, and the pageantry, spectacle, and bruising blows of NFL combat get the 69,143 fans inside Nissan Stadium cheering loudly. A flyover by aircraft from the Army's nearby Fort Campbell occasionally adds to the excitement. The stadium is on the opposite side of the Cumberland River from the honky-tonks and restaurants of Lower Broadway, a distance traversed on the Seigenthaler Bridge, one of the longest pedestrian bridges in the world.

1 Titans Way, 615-565-4200 (ticket office)
titansonline.com

TIP

Watch for developments about replacing Nissan Stadium. Plans for a $600 million renovation of the stadium built in 1999 blossomed into designs for a completely new facility just next door. The price of a new stadium perhaps nice enough to attract a Super Bowl? Somewhere north of $2 billion.

BARE YOUR FANG FINGERS
AT THE NASHVILLE PREDATORS

Skeptics wondered whether the NHL could succeed in the football-crazy South, but the Nashville Predators skated into Nashville in 1998, proved them wrong, and taught local broadcasters how to pronounce the names of Finnish, Russian, and Czech players. A Predators game is a Music City spectacle. A live band performs between periods, every National Anthem singer is stellar (sometimes it really is an A-List country star), the team mascot rappels from the rafters, and the crowd noise rattles the roof. (It's OK to bring earplugs.) Let your hair down and join the chants from the rowdies in Section 303. You'll soon beg for the visiting team to draw a penalty so you can raise two fingers on each hand and holler "Fang Fingers!" as the offender enters the penalty box. The taunts directed at visiting goalies who allow goals are even harsher.

501 Broadway, 615-770-7825
nhl.com/predators

TIP

Look for a display case on the Bridgestone Arena's 100 level that contains a 9-inch fang from a smilodon, a prehistoric saber-tooth cat. It was found in the 1971 excavation of a nearby building and became the inspiration for the hockey team's name.

GET DRESSY
AT THE STEEPLECHASE

The one-day Iroquois Steeplechase every May attracts two types: the horse set and the party set. Some people actually might be in both camps. For some, this springtime tradition since 1941 is about top-caliber racing horses. For others, this is an excuse to dress up in spring finery, flirt, drink outdoors, and see and be seen. It's part race, part fashion show, and part society soiree, a day for big flower-topped hats, sundresses, seersucker suits, bowties, and suspenders. Veteran attendees also know it's a day for sunscreen, patience returning to your car, and raingear. The three-mile track is in Percy Warner Park, and attendance can approach 25,000. Getting gussied up isn't a requirement, and general admission tickets are moderately priced. Rest assured that you can pay much more to get fancy food, adult beverages, and the shade of a hospitality tent. Proceeds ($10 million over the years) go to a good cause, the Monroe Carrel Jr. Children's Hospital at Vanderbilt.

2500 Old Hickory Blvd., 615-591-2991
iroquoissteeplechase.org

CLIMB THE STONE STEPS
INTO PERCY WARNER PARK

One of Nashville's most identifiable sights is the massive stone staircase that rises at the end of mansion-lined Belle Meade Boulevard and disappears into the forest of Percy Warner Park. If you huff and puff to the top, your reward comes when you turn around to look down the boulevard and see the Nashville skyline in the distance. Most Nashvillians simply call this spot "the stone steps," but its official name is the Allée. It was built during the Great Depression and is one of several gateways into the 3,180 acres of Percy Warner Park and companion Edwin Warner Park. Together, they are one of the biggest municipal park properties in the nation. At the top of the Allée, there's a moderately strenuous 2.5-mile hike on the Warner Woods Trail. Elsewhere, the parks offer more trails, equestrian paths, picnic areas, a great nature center, one-way driving routes, a golf course, and other ways to enjoy Mother Nature.

End of Belle Meade Blvd., 615-352-6299
nashville.gov/parks-and-recreation/parks/warner-parks.aspx

TRY TO RUN
13.1 OR 26.2 MILES

Nashville has several long-distance runs, but the big one is the St. Jude Rock 'n' Roll Nashville Marathon and Half-Marathon in April. Approximately 35,000 otherwise sane people pack onto Broadway and proceed to run, lope, shuffle, waddle, or walk through downtown, out Music Row, across the Cumberland River, and to points beyond before finishing at Nissan Stadium. The Nashville twist is that there are live bands on performance stages all along the route. A treat is seeing spectators' handheld signs of encouragement and humor. Among our favorites: "You can make it. I think." and "Remember that you paid to do this." Lots of money gets raised for St. Jude Children's Hospital, and runners get a big-name concert at Bridgestone Arena—after showering.

runrockroll.com/nashville

GO REALLY RETRO
AT DONELSON BOWL

Is a business really retro if its appearance is almost as it was in 1960 when it opened and not the modern creation of a designer with a flair for nostalgia? You can ponder that when stepping into the past at Donelson Bowl, a neighborhood bowling alley that has changed little since it opened. However, don't get too wrapped up in thoughts of *The Big Lewbowski*. Instead, select a bowling ball and head to your assigned lane (there are 24), and start having fun in today's world. Don't forget that beer and bowling go nicely together. The funky shoes, the laughter, and the camaraderie blend together to create great memories—and then there's the visceral pleasure of hurling a heavy object down a hardwood lane and knocking those bowling pins all over the place.

117 Donelson Pike, 615-883-3313
facebook.com/pg/bowl.in.donelson

TIP
Check Pinewood Social for a quite different bowling experience. It has six reclaimed lanes along with a restaurant, bar, coffee lounge, bocce ball court, and occasional yoga sessions. pinewoodsocial.com

MARVEL AT
A CLOUDED LEOPARD
AT THE NASHVILLE ZOO AT GRASSMERE

All of the Nashville Zoo at Grassmere's 325 animal species are special, but one is extra, extra special—clouded leopards. The secretive felines are among the world's rarest cats. Perhaps only 10,000 exist in the wild in tropical lowlands of Southeast Asia, which makes the Nashville Zoo's breeding program super important. The first successful artificial insemination was in 1992, and zoos around the world now use breeding and rearing techniques pioneered here. As cute as clouded leopards are, they are far from the zoo's only stars. Red pandas, meerkats, Mexican spider monkeys, and ring-tailed lemurs deliver more cuteness. The 100-acre zoo is a beauty and has earned international design recognition from the Association of Zoos & Aquariums for its Andean bear and Sumatran tiger habitats. In addition to its open-air habitats for animals and shaded walkways for visitors, it offers some high-energy attractions such as a 4D theater and the Soaring Eagle zip line. The Soaring Eagle ride starts up in the trees 110 feet off the ground, but don't expect to see any clouded leopards on your ride. They're too shy.

3777 Nolensville Pike, 615-833-1534
nashvillezoo.org

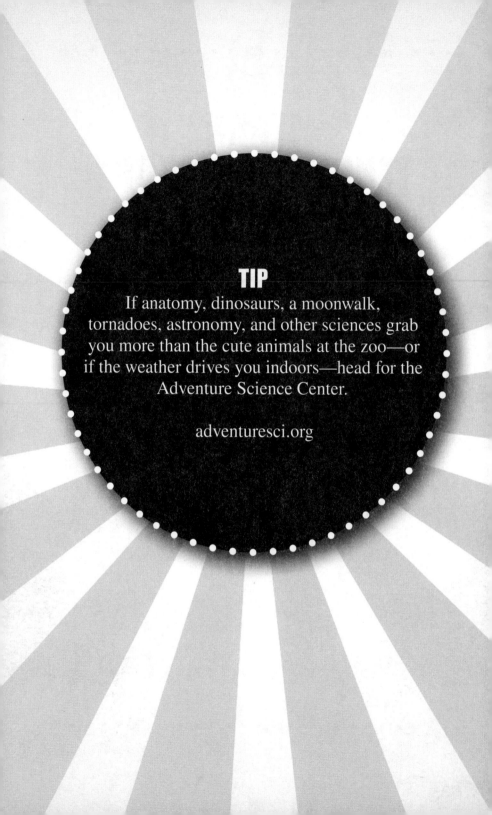

TIP

If anatomy, dinosaurs, a moonwalk, tornadoes, astronomy, and other sciences grab you more than the cute animals at the zoo—or if the weather drives you indoors—head for the Adventure Science Center.

adventuresci.org

LEARN TENNESSEE HISTORY
AT BICENTENNIAL MALL

Tennessee has the best history classroom in the world—it's all outdoors, has a grand view of the state capitol building, is next to the Nashville Farmers' Market for picnic supplies, and offers a 95-bell carillon that serenades you with "Tennessee Waltz." You can't do better than that. Officially it is the Bicentennial Capitol Mall State Park. Yep, it's a state park in the middle of the city. Its 19 acres of Tennessee time travel feature the decade-by-decade Pathway of History, the Court of Three Stars honoring Tennessee musical legends, a powerful World War II memorial, a 2,000-seat amphitheater popular for weddings, and the aforementioned carillon. Because this is a state park, park rangers lead informative walks in warm-weather months.

600 James Robertson Pkwy., 615-741-5280
tnstateparks.com/parks/about/bicentennial-mall

GLIDE THROUGH TOWN
ON AN ELECTRIC BICYCLE

When the weather is nice and you want to see Nashville from a different perspective, grab an electric bike from a BCycle rack and pedal your way to freedom. Glide around Centennial Park (use the Parthenon as the background for a selfie), explore Music Row (wave to the unresponsive naked dancers in the Musica sculpture) or be one with nature on miles of paved paths in Shelby Bottoms. The cost is modest (pay hourly or with a three-day or monthly pass). The beauty is that there are 30 automated BCycle kiosks scattered throughout town. Ditch your bike at any rack, then visit a museum, enjoy lunch, or explore a neighborhood on foot. After that, check out another set of wheels. BCycles have baskets, front and rear lights, and, yes, a bell—just like when you were a kid. (Here's a special hint: if you have a Nashville Public Library card, ask to check out a BCycle pass for a week.)

nashville.bcycle.com

TIP

Bicyclists love Nashville's greenway system, and Bike the Greenway at Wave Country in Donelson has rental bikes for exploring Shelby Bottoms in one direction or riding to Percy Priest Dam in the other. For details: bikethegreenway.net

---

TAKE A LAZY FLOAT
ON THE HARPETH RIVER

You could put a canoe into the Harpeth River and float all the way to New Orleans (that's if you turn left at the Cumberland, left at the Ohio, and left at the Mississippi), but you don't want to do that. What you do want to do is rent a canoe or kayak from Tip-a-Canoe or another outfitter for a point-to-point float on this easy Class I river. Its surroundings are rural rather than wild, a pleasant contrast from nearby developed Nashville. The Harpeth is quite popular with canoeists and kayakers, so you're unlikely ever to be truly alone. One popular float includes the Narrows of the Harpeth, a five-mile stretch where the river makes a huge bend and comes back within a quarter-mile of itself. Harpeth River State Park has nine access points along 40 miles of the river. Use sunscreen!

Harpeth River State Park
615-952-2099
tnstateparks.com/about/harpeth-river

Tip-a-Canoe
800-550-5810
tip-a-canoe.com

TIP

Not too many years ago, Nashvillians would call you crazy if you asked about kayaking downtown on the Cumberland River. No more. Nature paddles along Shelby Park and skyline paddles under the downtown bridges are popular outings these days. Cumberland Kayak is one outfitter.

cumberlandkayakadventure.com

BRING YOUR SWIMMING SUIT
TO THE STATE CAPITOL

Tennessee is blessed with many rivers, and you can get wet in 31 of them at the foot of Capitol Hill—at least figuratively. The Rivers of Tennessee Fountains in Bicentennial Mall State Park have fountainheads for each of those rivers in a delightful splash park where the young and the young at heart frolic, squeal, and shout. If the legislature is in session, there might be a different kind of shouting inside the capitol building, but that's not your concern as you race from the Watauga River in the mountains to the Elk River in the middle of the state to the Hatchie River out west. The Rivers of Tennessee Fountains are just steps away from a ground-level, 200-foot-long granite map of Tennessee. By the time you walk from Mountain City to Nashville, you'll probably be dry—and perhaps ready for another splash in the fountains after reaching Memphis.

600 James Robertson Pkwy., 615-741-5280
tnstateparks.com/parks/about/bicentennial-mall

CRUISE THE CUMBERLAND
ABOARD THE *GENERAL JACKSON* SHOWBOAT

Mark Twain, who was a riverboat pilot as well as a novelist and humorist, would feel right at home aboard the *General Jackson* showboat. Nashville architect Charles Warterfield made sure of that as he designed the 274-foot-long floating theater. Yes, diesel engines drive the paddlewheel, and there are modern electronics, but the showboat's pilots need to know every bend, curve, and nuance of the Cumberland River as they take up to a thousand passengers on 14-mile excursions from the Opryland area to downtown. The heart of the boat is a theater and dining room, but many passengers say the joy of the multi-deck *General Jackson* is seeing the Cumberland River from a new perspective. The *General Jackson*, which began cruising in 1985, is named for the first steamboat on the Cumberland River.

2812 Opryland Dr., 615-458-3900
generaljackson.com

TAKE IN
SOME COLLEGE BASEBALL

Nashville loves its minor league Nashville Sounds baseball team, but it's possible Nashville baseball fans follow college action even more. One reason is the Vanderbilt Commodores (national champions in 2014 and 2019) and all of the SEC powerhouses they play at Hawkins Field. Another is the rivalry between Belmont University and Lipscomb University, institutions separated by about two miles and a few points of theology. (Belmont has Southern Baptist roots, and Lipscomb is a Church of Christ school.) Toss Trevecca University, Tennessee State University, and nearby Middle Tennessee State University into the mix, and you see how easy it is to welcome spring's warm weather from the bleachers of a college baseball stadium.

vucommodores.com/sports/baseball
belmontbruins.com/sports/baseball
lipscombsports.com/sports/baseball
tnutrojans.com/sports/bsb
goblueraiders.com/sports/baseball

PEER INTO THE HEAVENS
AT DYER OBSERVATORY

Considering all of today's city lights, Nashville may seem an odd place for an astronomical observatory, but Vanderbilt Dyer Observatory south of downtown has been around since 1953, and Vanderbilt University's interest in astronomy dates to 1875. Numerous ways to see science at work dot the Dyer calendar— open house days, telescope nights, and (don't say you're surprised) concerts and other musical events. One of them is Bluebird on the Mountain, songwriter sessions in association with the famed Bluebird Cafe that start outdoors at sunset and end with views through the observatory's telescopes after dark. This means you can see a guitar-playing Nashville star and then some celestial stars on the same evening. As a bonus, you can chat with a university astronomer about all things celestial.

1000 Oman Dr., 615-373-4897
dyer.vanderbilt.edu

TIP
The Barnard-Seyfert Astronomical Society (named for two astronomers with ties to Nashville) organizes monthly stargazing events. Amateur astronomers set up telescopes and invite you to look into space.
bsasnashville.com

GO WILDERNESS HIKING
WHILE STILL IN TOWN

What became Tennessee's first official state natural area is in an unlikely location—just eight miles south of the capitol building and inside Nashville's city limits. It almost became an enclave of high-priced homes, but forward-thinking preservationists helped create the 1,367-acre Radnor Lake State Park and Natural Area. The centerpiece of this patch of wilderness is an 85-acre lake the Louisville & Nashville Railroad built in 1914 to supply water to steam locomotives. The lake and hilly habitat support beavers, ospreys, deer, wild turkeys, and more. There are nine miles of hiking trails, an aviary education center for non-releasable birds (including a bald eagle), a 50-seat amphitheater for ranger-led programs, and benches for silent solitude. Hiking, bird watching, and nature photography are the big attractions.

1160 Otter Creek Rd., 615-373-3467
tnstateparks.com/parks/about/radnor-lake

TIP

Beaman Park, another rugged state natural area diagonally across Davidson County, provides additional outdoor activity. Its 1,678 acres of ridges, valleys, forest, and creeks are part of the Highland Rim that surrounds Middle Tennessee. It was the largest gift of land ever to Nashville's park system.

CULTURE
AND HISTORY

LEARN HISTORY, LOVE MUSIC
AT THE RYMAN AUDITORIUM

You say the Ryman Auditorium looks more like a church than one of the world's most loved concert venues? You're right, because it opened its doors in 1892 as the Union Gospel Tabernacle, an ecumenical church inspired by the powerful preaching of evangelist Sam Jones and largely funded by a riverboat captain named Tom Ryman. Jones preached Ryman's funeral and proposed changing the name to the Ryman Auditorium, and the red brick building became the location for appearances by everyone from Teddy Roosevelt, Enrico Caruso, Sarah Bernhardt, and George Washington Carver to the Metropolitan Opera, W. C. Fields, Katharine Hepburn, and Bob Hope. Learn the story of promoter Lula C. Naff, who kept the building vibrant for decades, and about the full-time residence of the Grand Ole Opry from 1943 to 1974.

116 Rep. John Lewis Way N, 615-889-3060
ryman.com

TIP

The Ryman's history lesson is great, but go for some music. The theater returned from the dead in 1994 after a multi-million dollar project that preserved its extraordinary acoustics and original pews. It's fine to bring a seat cushion. The Grand Ole Opry is here occasionally, and artists of many genres fill other dates. Think Lizzo, Harry Styles, Wu-Tang Clan, Neil Diamond, Bruce Springsteen, James Brown, Kesha, R.E.M., and the Foo Fighters among many others.

QUICK, GET TO THE FRIST ART MUSEUM
BEFORE THINGS CHANGE

The Frist Art Museum is unlike most art museums. It has no permanent collection. Instead, it is a venue for an ever-changing series of exhibitions and special events that spotlight art from around the world in an imposing, historic art deco building that once was Nashville's main post office. Exhibitions about American art from World War I, images from Nashville's Civil Rights struggle, or contemporary Asian art are interspersed with artifacts from ancient Egypt, Parisian fashion, or iconic European sports cars. Highly popular is the Martin ArtQuest Gallery, with interactive stations, where you can make a print, paint a watercolor, or create your own short animation. This gallery is included in adult admission. (Kids 18 and younger are always admitted to the museum free of charge.)

919 Broadway, 615-244-3340
fristartmuseum.org

TIP
The Frist's gift shop is well known as the place for truly artful gifts. Find prints, books, blown glass, jewelry, and other creations of local and regional artisans.

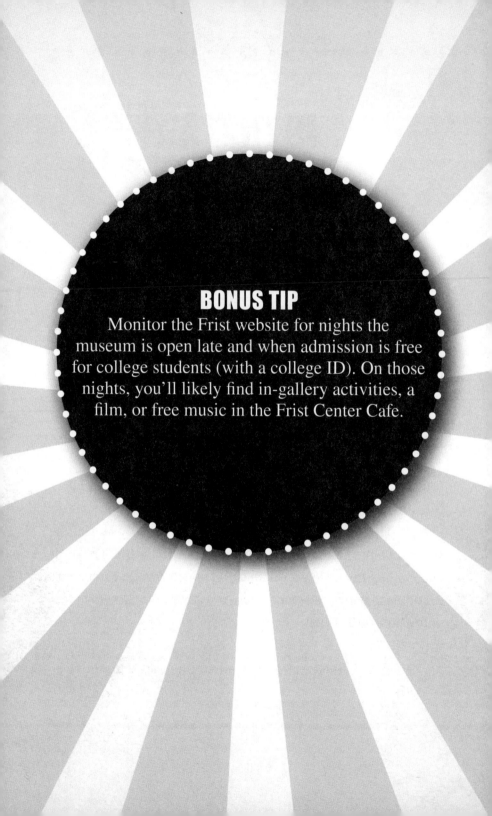

BONUS TIP

Monitor the Frist website for nights the museum is open late and when admission is free for college students (with a college ID). On those nights, you'll likely find in-gallery activities, a film, or free music in the Frist Center Cafe.

IS THAT A ROLLER COASTER OR WHAT?

Many a Nashville visitor has peered across the Cumberland River from Lower Broadway and pondered, "Is that a roller coaster over there?" Well, no—it's a piece of attention-getting public art called "Ghost Ballet for the East Bank Machineworks," and it's as good a starting point as any to explore more than 50 pieces of public art scattered across the city. Some are super-realistic, such as the naked (and we mean really naked) 15-foot-tall dancers in "Musica" at Music Row. Some are sobering and thought-provoking, such as "Witness Walls" at Public Square Park. Some are humorous, such as a bike rack called "Handlebar Moustache" in East Nashville and another bike rack that looks like a sliced tomato near the Farmers' Market. Since this is Music City, scout out the life-sized bronze of Country Music Hall of Fame member Chet Atkins at the corner of Fifth Avenue North and Union Street. He's strumming on a guitar while perched on a stool, and there's an empty stool next to him for you to sit for your photo with a star.

Almost everywhere you look
metroartsnashville.com/metro-public-art-collection

● ●

SEE NASHVILLE'S CIVIL WAR HISTORY
AT FORT NEGLEY

Nashville hasn't done a particularly good job telling its Civil War story, but that's not for lack of a good venue. Fort Negley, the largest inland fort built during the war, looms over I-65, and thousands of people zoom by it every day without realizing it, much less planning a visit. Those who do stroll its expansive grounds learn multiple stories about the war. The Confederacy surrendered Nashville early in the war, and the Union immediately began making it the most fortified city in the nation except for Washington, DC, itself. More than 2,700 laborers (people who had escaped slavery or already were free) did the work. Between 600 and 800 died, and only 310 received pay. The fort deteriorated over the decades, the Civilian Conservation Corps did restoration work on it during the Depression, and more restoration and interpretation have occurred in recent years. It now is a Nashville park with an excellent visitor center. This piece of American history awaits your exploration.

1100 Fort Negley Blvd., 615-862-8470
nashville.gov/departments/parks/historic-sites/fort-negley

LEARN A FULLER CIVIL WAR STORY
IN FRANKLIN

After the 2015 racial murders inside the Mother Emanuel A.M.E. Church in Charleston, South Carolina, and the 2017 white nationalist Unite the Right rally in Charlottesville, Virginia, community leaders in the Nashville-adjacent town of Franklin re-examined their community's Civil War history. Franklin was the site of a major battle in 1864, and its modern tourism focused largely on the fighting, not the realities of a slave-holding society. A statue of an anonymous Confederate soldier remains on the town square. Four men—two Black and two white—advocated for what became "The Fuller Story." Now, five historical markers surround the Confederate monument and address the inhumanity of slavery, the toll of war, and the unachieved goals of Reconstruction. More importantly, "The Fuller Story" added a statue on the square. It depicts a Black Union soldier—a member of the United States Colored Troops—and honors 200,000 formerly enslaved people who enlisted in the Union army. More than 20,000 were from Tennessee, and 300 were from the Franklin area.

visitfranklin.com/fuller-story-project

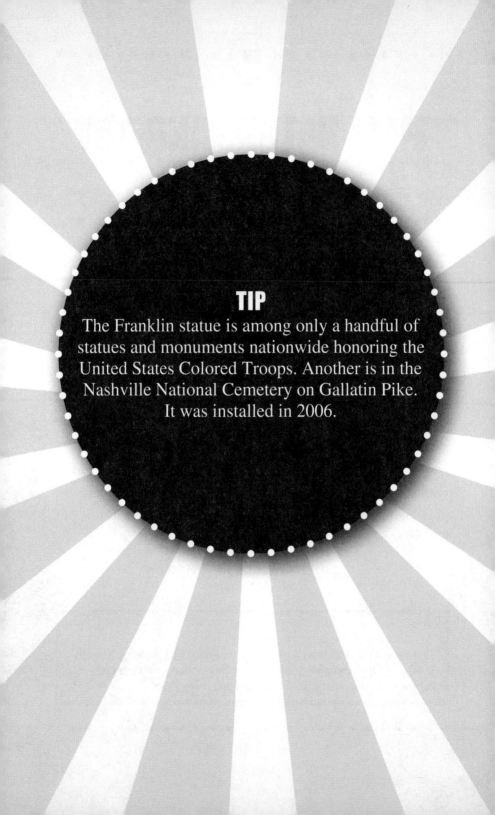

TIP

The Franklin statue is among only a handful of statues and monuments nationwide honoring the United States Colored Troops. Another is in the Nashville National Cemetery on Gallatin Pike. It was installed in 2006.

MEET NATURE AND ART
AT CHEEKWOOD

Unless seeing Elvis Presley's Graceland in Memphis is your thing, visiting an old mansion might not turn you on. Rethink that at Cheekwood Estate & Gardens. This showplace exists because of a 36-room Georgian-style mansion built with money from a grocery empire and Maxwell House Coffee (you know, "good to the last drop") that now houses an impressive art collection. The art is mostly American works from 1910 to 1970. That's all very nice, but most people are drawn in by the 55-acre estate's gardens, the spectacular outdoor art installations (think Dale Chihuly glass), the themed seasonal events, and the live music that seems to be everywhere in Nashville. The gardens burst with color every spring with 150,000 bulbs, autumn glows with 5,000 chrysanthemums, and Christmas means one million glowing lights along garden paths. Yes, it's an old mansion, but there's nothing dull about this place.

1200 Forrest Park Dr., 615-356-8000
cheekwood.org

TIP

Thursdays from May through October are special. Cheekwood's Thursday Night Out parties deliver live music, food, spirits, lawn games, wellness classes, garden strolls, and more.

LOOK OVERHEAD
AT TWO CLASSIC HOTELS

Step inside the Union Station Hotel or the Hermitage Hotel, and we guarantee you'll look up. These properties are from an era of grand hotels, and the lobby ceilings command your attention. The castle-like Union Station Hotel opened in 1900 to serve passengers on eight railroad lines, and its 65-foot-high barrel-vaulted ceiling accented with Tiffany-style stained glass marked it as a grand structure, indeed. Ten years later, the Beaux Arts–style Hermitage Hotel opened a few blocks away, and its soaring lobby pulled guests' eyes overhead to admire a ceiling of intricate ornamental plaster and painted glass. Over the decades, both buildings had their ups and downs, but they have been at the top of the hotel game for years. The modern chrome-and-glass design of new hotels is pretty, but these two gems are in a class of their own.

231 6th Ave. N, 615-244-3121
thehermitagehotel.com

1001 Broadway, 615-726-1001
unionstationhotelnashville.com

TIP
The art deco men's bathroom at the Hermitage Hotel is such a design hit that women often ask for a peek. How notable is it? It's in the America's Best Restroom Hall of Fame. No lie, there really is such a thing.

DISCOVER
TENNESSEE'S TREASURES
AT THE STATE MUSEUM

Tennessee became the 16th state in 1796 and immediately began accumulating stuff that later became artifacts in the Tennessee State Museum. Many of those items and the stories that go with them found a dedicated home in 2018 after decades of relative obscurity in the basement levels of a state office building. The museum now is a stand-alone, multi-story, $160-million building just north of the capitol building. Its neighbors are the Bicentennial Capitol Mall and the Farmers Market, so many more people are finding it. The museum offers several permanent exhibits and a full calendar of special displays and events. This is the place to see 10,000-year-old mastodon bones, President Andrew Johnson's own ticket to his impeachment trial, banners from the 1920 women's suffrage campaign, and even a jacket and skirt donated by entertainer Tina Turner. Tennessee has managed to collect a passel of interesting treasures since 1796.

1000 Rosa Parks Blvd., 615-741-2692
tnmuseum.org

EASE DOWN
THE NATCHEZ TRACE PARKWAY

The northern end of the 444-mile-long Natchez Trace Parkway is just west of Nashville, making an exploration of just a bit of this scenic route an easy and rewarding day trip. Within the first 50 miles or so are a double arch bridge over Tennessee Highway 96 (a perfect landmark for a post-worthy photo), a War of 1812 memorial, the two-story Gordon House (built in 1818 and once a place of respite for early travelers on the actual Natchez Trace), a hiking opportunity at Devil's Backbone State Natural Area, and a pretty waterfall on Swan Creek. You can augment your trip with a meal at the Loveless Cafe or a short detour for shopping at the village of Leiper's Fork. The parkway, where the speed limit is 50, is a two-lane blacktop that also is very popular with bicyclists. Go slowly and enjoy the scenery. If you keep driving, you'll soon be in Alabama and then Mississippi, having followed the hunting and trading route of Native Americans and early pioneer settlers.

800-305-7417
nps.gov/natr

HUG A BOOK
AT THE SOUTHERN FESTIVAL OF BOOKS

When the Southern Festival of Books rolls around every October, the population of Legislative Plaza changes dramatically. Gone are the legislators, capitol staffers, lobbyists, and protestors or advocates for legislative bills. In their place are people who love, love, love books—all kinds of books, even ones that some people might someday want to ban. The book lovers come to interact with approximately 200 authors of local, regional, and national stature in a three-day extravaganza of readings, panel discussions, and book signings. This is Nashville, so live music is part of the mix, too. If you're feeling benevolent, you can dine with an author in the grandeur of the War Memorial Auditorium at the fundraising Authors in the Round Dinner and get that author's book to take home. The festival is a project of Humanities Tennessee, a nonprofit that promotes lifelong learning and civil discourse.

Legislative Plaza
6th Ave. N between Charlotte Ave. and Union St., 615-770-0006
sofestofbooks.org

CONTEMPLATE
AMERICA'S WORST TRAIN WRECK

If not for a marker along the Richland Creek Greenway, you'd likely never know that the worst train wreck in American history happened in Nashville. In 1918, the site was a cornfield. Today, it's a place where walkers, joggers, bicyclists, and parents with kids in strollers pass by in between a Publix supermarket and the Lion's Head Shopping Center. Human error put two passenger trains on a collision course at Dutchman's Curve, one traveling at 50 mph and the other at 60 mph. The crash, which killed at least 101 and injured at least 171, was heard two miles away. More than 50,000 people came to help, search for survivors, or simply to see the scene of tragedy. Reading the marker gives you plenty to contemplate as you traverse the 4.8 miles of this quiet and peaceful greenway.

Off White Bridge Pike
greenwaysfornashville.org

TOUR THE CAPITOL
THAT BECAME A CIVIL WAR FORT

Putting all political sarcasm aside, Tennessee's capitol is a beautiful building worth visiting. William Strickland, an architectural and engineering rock star of his time and a leader in Greek Revival design, was the architect of the statehouse, which was finished in 1859. (Tour trivia: Strickland died during construction and is buried in the north facade.) Part of his inspiration was the Monument of Lysicrates from 334 B.C. Athens, perhaps a foreshadowing Nashville's construction of a replica of the Parthenon at the end of the century. When Union troops occupied Nashville early in the Civil War, the capitol building became Fortress Andrew Johnson, but its cannons never were fired in anger. Guided tours lasting 45 minutes occur six times a day Monday through Friday (no reservation needed for groups smaller than 12).

Charlotte Ave. between 6th Ave. and 7th Ave. N, 615-741-0830
capitol.tn.gov/about/capitolvisit.html

TIP
Downtown Presbyterian Church at 154 5th Avenue North is another building Strickland designed (page 100). It's the only church with an Egyptian motif you're ever likely to see.

TRY TO FIGURE OUT ANDREW JACKSON
AT THE HERMITAGE

The legacy of President Andrew Jackson lies somewhere between perplexing and polarizing. He was a frontiersman and a man of the people, but he owned slaves. He saw the specter of secession and resisted it, but he was the force behind the infamous Trail of Tears. He paid down the national debt to zero, but that precipitated a financial crisis. He was stunningly important in American history, and his complex, intriguing, and sometimes agonizing life is the focus of the Hermitage, his retreat and refuge that many historians call the best-preserved early presidential home. Every ticket gets you into the excellent "Andrew Jackson: Born for a Storm" museum exhibit (don't miss the video presentation simply called "Jackson") and access to gardens, grounds, and the tomb where Jackson and his beloved wife Rachel are buried. An enhanced ticket provides an interpreter-led tour inside the mansion. Stories of those who were enslaved at the Hermitage are illuminated in a special tour called "In Their Footsteps: Lives of the Hermitage Enslaved."

4580 Rachel's Ln., 615-889-2941
thehermitage.com

MARVEL
AT AN EGYPTIAN-MOTIF PRESBYTERIAN CHURCH

Amid all the hoopla of downtown, there is at least one quiet refuge with a historical twist that's very much worth visiting. It's the third incarnation of Downtown Presbyterian Church, and its architectural style is Egyptian Revival. There's a good chance you never learned about this style in your art history class, but it was inspired by Napoleon's conquest of Egypt and was popular for a while in the 1800s. Famous Philadelphia architect William Strickland designed the church as a side gig while dealing with a bigger project, Tennessee's capitol building. In addition to the Egyptian motif, a tour highlight is the church's 2,709-pipe organ. Check the website for tour dates, and consider showing up some Sunday morning, if only to hear the organ. The congregation dates to 1814 (Presidents Jackson and Polk were worshippers), and it is a mainstay in ministry to the homeless and urban poor. You are welcome to volunteer Saturday mornings to help serve a community breakfast.

154 Rep. John Lewis Way N, 615-254-7584
dpchurch.com

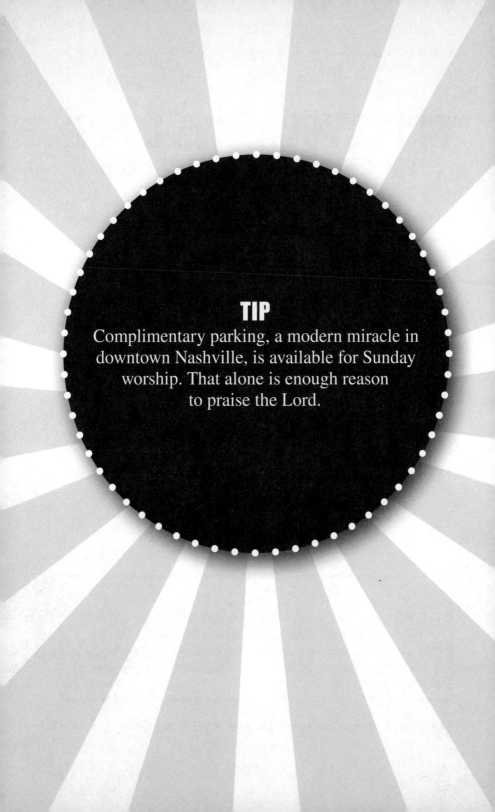

TIP

Complimentary parking, a modern miracle in downtown Nashville, is available for Sunday worship. That alone is enough reason to praise the Lord.

BRING YOUR OWN CHAIR
FOR SHAKESPEARE IN THE PARK

The August and September tradition of Summer Shakespeare is into its fourth decade of outdoor performances. These are casual events in the sense that you bring your own blanket or lawn chairs, and admission is free. However, a $10 donation to the Nashville Shakespeare Festival (NSF) is thoroughly appreciated, and if you want an upgraded experience, special packages to purchase include tables, chairs, and a picnic dinner. Remember that this is Music City, so arrive an hour before curtain time for a concert from one of the area's budding artists. The Nashville Shakespeare Festival also has winter productions, which blessedly are indoors. Like Shakespeare in his day, NSF executive artistic director Denice Hicks is a local theater legend, so seeing one of her productions is oh-so-Nashville.

8 City Blvd., 615-255-2273
nashvilleshakes.org

TIP

Check the NSF winter calendar for "Abbreviated Shakespeare" (*Macbeth* in 60 minutes or *Romeo and Juliet* is 75 minutes, for instance). Also, "Shakespeare Allowed!" is a public reading of an entire play the first Saturday of the month at the Downtown Public Library. The readers are anyone who shows up.

FEEL REGAL
AT THE SCHERMERHORN
SYMPHONY CENTER

If Nashville had real royalty instead of country music royalty, their palace would look like the Schermerhorn Symphony Center. This $123.5-million neoclassical beauty opened in 2006 as home to the Nashville Symphony, one of America's most active recording orchestras and winner of more than a dozen Grammy Awards. Its 1,800-seat Laura Turner Concert Hall has a mechanical system able to flip from concert seating to a ballroom configuration in less than two hours, and hearing its 3,500-pipe concert organ is a pure joy. As palatial as it is, it is not intimidating. People who never have attended a classical concert have enjoyed special nights when performers such as Sheryl Crow, Tony Bennett, Diana Ross, Willie Nelson, Alabama, and the Beach Boys have appeared—in joint performance with the Nashville Symphony.

1 Symphony Pl., 615-687-6400
nashvillesymphony.org

TIP
The 1,727-seat Fisher Center at Belmont University is another eye-popping Nashville concert venue to check out. thefishercenter.com

WELL,
OUR PARTHENON HAS A ROOF

Tell your globetrotting friends they can save themselves a trip to Greece, because they can see what the Parthenon originally looked like in Centennial Park. Yep, that's a full-scale replica of the Athenian temple at Centennial Park in midtown Nashville, and ours has a roof that protects a 42-foot-tall statue of Athena. A 6-foot-tall Mercury stands on her outstretched palm. The building exists as a second-generation leftover from the Tennessee Centennial Exposition in 1897. The Parthenon built for the exposition was made of plaster and lathe and gradually deteriorated, but the city loved having a Parthenon and built the current concrete structure in 1925. An $11-million sprucing-up of Centennial Park, which created clear sightlines and brightened the night view with LED lights, wrapped up in 2021.

2500 West End Ave., 615-862-8431
conservancyonline.com

TIP

To see a towering rendering of the 1897 Tennessee Centennial Exposition and a dozen other historic Nashville scenes, check out the murals near the Tennessee Ballroom of the Gaylord Opryland Hotel.

TAKE YOUR PICK
OF NASHVILLE ART CRAWLS

You don't even have to like art shows to enjoy the art crawl scene in Nashville. Of course, it helps to appreciate others' artistic skills, but Nashville's art crawls are opportunities to visit different parts of town, consider many art media, and usually get handed a free glass of wine and maybe a chunk of cheese. What's not to like? Here are two art crawls and an art stumble to check out. All three are free.

Explore a variety of downtown galleries, plus places such as Hatch Show Print and Downtown Presbyterian Church, on the First Saturday Art Crawl Downtown. Stray off the route just a bit for the 21c Museum Hotel.

If you don't want to go downtown, an alternative on the same Saturday night each month is the WeHo Art Crawl in the Wedgewood-Houston neighborhood. More than a dozen stops include galleries, artist-run collectives, and maker spaces.

Often funky East Nashville calls its event the East Nashville Art Stumble on the second Saturday each month. Destinations are scattered through East Nashville and into the Inglewood neighborhood.

800-657-6910
visitmusiccity.com/things-to-do-in-nashville/attractions/art-scene/art-crawls

PONDER 550 OIL CHANGES
AT LANE MOTOR MUSEUM

Every one of the 550 distinctive automobiles at the Lane Motor Museum gets an annual oil change and tune-up. LMM specializes in European cars, many of which will be new to you. Non-European models are from Asia, South America, and North America. Of note are the tiniest production car ever built, the Peel P50 from the Isle of Man, which at 53 inches long is shorter than Brenda Lee is tall; the propeller-driven Helicron from France; and the 1942 German Tatra, a car on skis the Nazis wanted to drive across the Russian steppes. About 150 vehicles are on the main display floor every day. While you can't touch them, you can walk around them and admire from every angle. One treasure is museum owner Jeff Lane's 1955 MG TF-1500. He began restoring it at age 12 and took his driver's license test in it.

702 Murfreesboro Pike, 615-742-7445
lanemotormuseum.org

TIP

If the main floor's cars aren't enough, ask about "vault tours" to a lower level for more museum inventory and about Museum Fun Days that feature vehicle demonstrations and limited opportunities for rides.

DISCOVER ART
AT FISK UNIVERSITY

If ever a city had an underappreciated treasure, it is Nashville's Carl Van Vechten Gallery at Fisk University. The gallery occupies a building completed in 1889 as the first gymnasium at any predominantly Black college in America. Any hint of its athletic past is long gone, replaced by three centuries of extraordinary artwork, mostly from an array of African-American and African artists. The gallery owns 4,000 pieces, so only a small percentage is shown at any one time. Among its holdings is the 101-piece Stieglitz Collection of Modern Art (Picasso, Cezanne, Renoir, and more), a gift from Stieglitz's widow, artist Georgia O'Keeffe. Fisk and the Crystal Bridges Museum in Bentonville, Arkansas, share ownership of the Stieglitz Collection, which rotates between them every two years.

1000 17th Ave. N, 615-329-8720
fiskuniversitygalleries.org

TIP

Slip next door to Cravath Hall, and climb the stairs to the second floor to admire a set of murals by Aaron Douglas, a key artist of the Harlem Renaissance and the founding chair of Fisk's art department. Jubilee Hall is another Fisk jewel.

GET SOULFUL
ON THE "ORIGINAL MUSIC ROW"

As far back as the 1920s and 1930s, Jefferson Street was alive with music, but it wasn't country music. Jefferson Street was the heartbeat of a thriving, but segregated, Black section of Nashville, and the music that evolved there had national impact. It was R&B and jazz heaven. Nightspots including the Del Morocco Club, Club Baron, and Ann's Place reverberated with the music of Marion James, Etta James, Little Richard, and a young Jimmy (later Jimi) Hendrix. Construction of Interstate 40 decimated that scene and altered the entire community. Nashville native Lorenzo Washington wanted to preserve that history and in 2011 opened the Jefferson Street Sound Museum in what once was a boarding house. It's casual, a labor of love, and a treasured piece of Music City's history. Stop in to see the place Ray Charles came by to pick up his sax player, Hank Crawford.

2004 Jefferson St.
jeffersonstreetsound.com

LEARN CONSTITUTIONAL AND CIVIL RIGHTS HISTORY
AT THE LIBRARY

Permanent exhibitions at the Nashville Public Library honor earthshattering events. The Votes for Women Room explains how Tennessee was the deciding state to ratify the 19th Amendment to the US Constitution, securing women's right to vote. A decades-long struggle came down to just one Tennessee legislator—who changed his negative vote to "yea" after receiving a letter from his mother. Nearby is the Civil Rights Room that illuminates the Civil Rights turmoil of the 1950s and 1960s and how well-trained, dedicated, peaceful students from four Black colleges and universities changed the structure of Nashville. The room overlooks Church St. and Seventh Ave. North, a focal point for segregated lunch counter protests. The centerpiece is a circular table resembling a lunch counter. Perch on a stool and read about students' resolve to end injustice, and then examine 14 powerful newspaper photos from the era, especially ones showing angry adults screaming at little first-graders on their way to school. The experience gives you pause.

615 Church St., 615-862-5800
library.nashville.org

PICKIN' AND PRINTIN'

$25

IN NASHVILLE TENN SINCE 1879.

Hatch Show Print Nashville Tennessee

© 2017 Hatch Show Print

THAN THE COOLEST SPOT IN TOWN

HATCH SHOW PRINT
★★★ NASHVILLE, TENNESSEE ★★★

COPYRIGHT 2015 ◆ HATCH SHOW PRINT

YOU'RE JUST MY WOOD TYPE

$1

© 2015 Hatch Show Print

$15

Hatch SHOW PRINT

SINCE 1879

HATCH SHOW PRINT © 2011

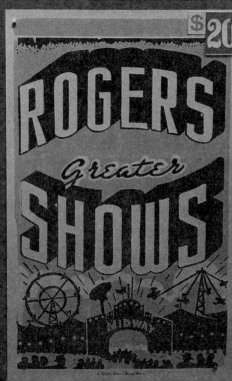

$20

ROGERS GREATER SHOWS

MIDWAY

© 2011 Hatch Show Print

SHOPPING
AND FASHION

BUY SOME OLD STUFF
ON AN ANTIQUING TRIP

Eighth Avenue south of downtown used to be heaven for antique hunters, with multiple malls and shops offering everything from fine antique furniture to mid-century modern home furnishing to, well, items some would call junk and others would call treasures. Recent real estate shifts meant relocation or closure for most of them, but quality Nashville antiquing expeditions remain plentiful. You can find truly high-end items at the GasLamp Antiques in the 100 Oaks area and troves of decorating items and collectibles at East Nashville Antiques & Vintage on Gallatin Road, Music Valley Antiques & Marketplace near the Grand Ole Opry House, and the Goodlettsville Antique Mall in the RiverGate area. The fun is in the hunt. You may just find that *Hee Haw* lunch box your mom once discarded.

TIP
If the antique hunting bug truly has bitten you, you'll go nuts exploring more than 130 businesses that are members of a statewide antiquing organization. tennesseeantiquetrail.com

MEET LITTLE BERTHA
AT THE PEANUT SHOP

When the enticing aroma of roasting peanuts wafts through the wind tunnel that is the Nashville Arcade, that means Little Bertha is at work again. Little Bertha is the peanut-roasting machine in the Peanut Shop, a tiny store that has been pleasing customers since 1927. The friendliness of the owners (two effervescent sisters) is as delightful as the peanut aroma. The Peanut Shop has much more than roasted peanuts. That's why you may find yourself saying, "I came for some peanuts, but I'll have some cashews, some of those Spanish reds, and how about some chocolate-covered almonds, too?" This is definitely old-school retailing. Bins of various varieties of nuts and other treats fill glass-fronted cases, and your orders are scooped out and weighed on the shop's original countertop scales. As low-key as the Peanut Shop might appear, it's up with the times and ships online orders around the world. The sisters report having big fans in England and Australia.

19 Arcade Alley, 615-256-3394
nashvillenut.com

EQUIP YOURSELF FOR THE OUTDOORS
AT FRIEDMAN'S

A neon soldier sign on 21st Avenue South tells you you've found Friedman's Army Navy Outdoor Store. It has been a destination since 1972 for camping gear, fishing tackle, hunting accessories, combat boots, hiking boots, rain boots, fleeces, raincoats, ponchos, binoculars, goggles, fishing and hunting licenses, and more—just about anything you'd ever need for work or fun in the outdoors. Some of the merchandise has that military-surplus look, but tags on other items say Timberland, Georgia Boot, Duckhead, Carhartt, Zebco, Rapala, Strike King, Tasco, Buck, and other top-quality name brands. The store is absolutely packed with merchandise, and it offers something you don't find at big-box outdoor stores—personal service in a locally owned and operated business.

2021 21st Ave. S, 615-297-3343
friedmansarmynavyoutdoorstore.net

SLOW DOWN
IN SOME SMALL TOWNS

A dozen small towns southwest of Nashville—none larger than 5,000 residents and most much smaller—joined hands to promote themselves collectively as Nashville's Big Back Yard (NBBY) and offer a huge variety of shopping opportunities. Among the bigger ones is Centerville, which claims country comedy legend Minnie Pearl as a favorite daughter. Mixed in with the shops on Centerville's town square is the chamber of commerce, where a live radio show, "The Grinders Switch Radio Hour," is broadcast every Saturday morning. You're welcome to join the "studio" audience and buy crafts and souvenirs of the region. Among the smallest NBBY communities is the village of Hampshire, where three wineries and the art-filled Copperhead Creek Studio await you. More shopping is in Linden, where the Buffalo River Artisans Co-op showcases artists who paint, weave, blow glass, and more. Also in Linden is the quaint 12-room Commodore Hotel, whose owners can arrange a kayak float for you on the Buffalo River.

nashvillesbigbackyard.org

BINGE ON BOOKS
AT MCKAY'S

Powell's Books is famous in Portland, Oregon, and Indy Reads is famous in Indianapolis, Indiana, but McKay's in Nashville is catching up with them as a great destination for used books. McKay's opened in Nashville in 2007 and is a veritable warehouse of "previously loved" books, music, movies, video games, and electronics. It doesn't deal in anything new. Everything on the shelves was brought by everyday folks—just like you—and traded for in-store acquisitions or cash. Up to 10,000 items flow into the store every day. It's a strictly in-person experience—no internet sales. McKay's in Nashville has a somewhat convoluted history, with sibling operations in Chattanooga and Knoxville, Tennessee, and in Greensboro and Winston-Salem, North Carolina. Of course, you can come in without having anything to trade. As management says, "Think of it as a treasure hunt."

636 Old Hickory Blvd., 615-353-2595
mckaybooks.com

BE SURPRISED
AT MARATHON VILLAGE

Marathon Village has a retail mix you'll not find at any shopping mall, strip center, or so-called lifestyle center. It's a jumble of businesses that coalesce to become a retail and entertainment destination in the shadow of an interstate highway yet practically off the radar. There are some big names, such as Jack Daniel's, Harley-Davidson (apparel, not motorcycles), and Antique Archaeology. Then there are smaller entities such as the Grinder's Switch Winery, Nashville Olive Oil Company, Screened Threads (a screen printing business), and Lorraine's Jewelry. Toss in Nashville Tactical Lounge (it calls itself a "high-end knife shop"), the Third Coast Comedy Club, and the Corsair Distillery and you begin to understand that you shouldn't try to guess what's next down the hall of this sprawling facility that was an automobile factory in the early 1900s. Developer Barry Walker saw possibilities no one else imagined, and he has managed to keep the industrial history of the complex alive.

1305 Clinton St., 615-327-1010
marathonvillage.net

BUY A POSTER
AT HATCH SHOW PRINT

Just as a rhinestone suit is Nashville's iconic stage outfit, the distinctive graphic artwork of a Hatch Show Print poster is Nashville's unmistakable souvenir. Hatch began creating entertainment posters in 1879, and it thrives to this day because it never abandoned its signature look and production method, which is oh-so-18th century. Artists use flat-bed presses, hand-carved blocks, and classic lettering to produce distinctive posters. They once did it for Roy Acuff, Hank Williams, and Elvis Presley, and they do it today for contemporary artists in all genres. (Most shows at the nearby Ryman Auditorium are the subject of a new print. Look for the Hatch gallery there.) The shop is part of the Country Music Hall of Fame and Museum, and you can peer through huge picture windows to see artists at work. Learn more on a guided tour. If you're gung-ho, sign up for a "Block Party," where you can make your own print, T-shirt, tote bag, or tea towel. Don't wear white that day.

224 Rep. John Lewis Way S, 615-256-2805
hatchshowprint.com

MEET AN ARTISAN
AT THE TENNESSEE CRAFT FAIR

It's no problem meeting a highly talented craft artisan at a Tennessee Craft Fair every May and October in Centennial Park. That's because participation in the fair requires artisans to stay on site. The three-day fairs will turn you green with envy if your best craft handiwork was a woven potholder or a plastic lanyard at summer camp. Centennial Park's Parthenon provides the backdrop—and perhaps artistic inspiration—for the artisans occupying tents that pop up like giant mushrooms. You can buy the works of juried, award-winning artists and crafters who work in clay, textiles, glass, paint, photography, and other media. Don't look for potholders and lanyards. Admission to both fairs is free.

Centennial Park, 2500 West End Ave.
tennesseecraft.org./events/craft-fairs

TIP

Early every October, Tennessee Craft Week schedules craft events across Tennessee. Find one that will inspire a road trip.
tennesseecraft.org/tennessee-craft-week

EXPLORE AN ARCADE
WITHOUT PINBALL MACHINES

Nashville's first shopping mall—and one of America's oldest—hides in plain sight between 4th Avenue North and Representative John Lewis Way North. It is the Nashville Arcade, built in 1902. The grand opening in 1903 drew 40,000 people when Nashville's total population was 125,000. In recent years, the Arcade's tenant mix has been the subject of speculation because of an ownership change, but optimists always hope for an eclectic combination of shops, restaurants, service businesses, and galleries. Whatever businesses are there have a gabled glass roof overhead, adding to a European flair, which makes sense because the original developers' inspiration was the Galleria Vittoria Emanuele II Arcade in Milan. The Arcade is most vibrant middays during the week, when it bustles with downtown workers and smart kids from nearby Hume-Fogg Academic Magnet High School, one of the nation's best prep schools.

65 Arcade Alley, 615-248-6673
en.wikipedia.org/wiki/Nashville_Arcade

BE A KID AGAIN
AT PHILLIPS TOY MART

Perhaps the only experience better than being a kid in a candy store is being a kid in a toy store. That delight has drawn kids, their parents, and their grandparents to Phillips Toy Mart since 1946. This family-owned business is packed almost to the ceiling with toys of all types—infant toys, yard toys, board games, toy cars and trucks, dolls, princess costumes, books for all ages, collectibles, and more. Regardless of your age, you'll stop to watch the model trains go around and around a make-believe community complete with a whirling carousel and an ice rink with skaters. Go ahead and at least buy a coloring book and some crayons.

5207 Harding Pike, 615-352-5363
phillipstoymart.com

GET GOOEY
WITH A GOO GOO CLUSTER

Not only can you satisfy your sweet tooth with a Goo Goo Cluster (a glorious round mound of caramel, marshmallow nougat, roasted peanuts, and milk chocolate), but you also can demonstrate your culinary creativity by designing your own Goo Goo at the Goo Goo Chocolate Co. The shop sells plenty of Goo Goos and related merchandise along with "experiences" such as the Secrets of Goo Goo (a chocolate and wine pairing event) and Goos & Booze (a chocolate and spirits tasting event). Both experiences include hands-on candy making as well as the tippling. The Taste of Goo Goo experience offers the candy making without the alcohol. This tasty treat gives Nashville another claim to fame, because Goo Goos were America's first combination candy bar. The sweet story started in 1912 and is going strong today.

116 3rd Ave. S, 615-490-6685
googoo.com

JOIN THE FAMILY
AT PARNASSUS BOOKS

Parnassus Books isn't just a suburban bookstore. It's a community center where books are sold, reading lists are shared, authors sign books, storytellers entertain children, and everybody gets a welcome wag from a greeter dog. Author Ann Patchett and her business partners opened Parnassus when Nashville's last independent bookstore closed. The idea of the Athens of the South not having an independent bookstore was more than they could bear. Parnassus really does make you feel welcome and like family, and its online magazine called "Musings" features Patchett's blog. When you buy one of Patchett's books online, she will personalize it if you just ask. By the way, the store's name comes from Mount Parnassus, the home of literature, learning, and music in Greek mythology.

3900 Hillsboro Pike, 615-953-2243
parnassusbooks.net

TIP

For a hard-to-find, out-of-print, used, or
rare volume, inquire at Elder's Bookstore
and Rhino Booksellers. Rhino also has vinyl
records and musical instruments.

Elder's Bookstore
101 White Bridge Rd., 615-352-1562
eldersbookstore.com

Rhino Booksellers
4918 Charlotte Ave., 615-297-0310
rhinobooksellers.com

SHARPEN YOUR NEGOTIATING SKILLS
AT THE NASHVILLE FLEA MARKET

Prior to the COVID-19 pandemic, the Nashville Flea Market drew half a million bargain hunters a year to prowl through the booths of between 800 and 1,200 vendors the fourth weekend of every month. (December's market dates, of course, are the third weekend to accommodate last-minute Christmas shoppers.) The flea market is working its way back up to that scale, but it's still a blast to inspect—and maybe make an impulse purchase from—the vast volume of antique furniture, clothing, carpets, jewelry, leather goods, yard art, knick-knacks, and, well, just stuff. The Nashville Flea Market action is at the Nashville Fairgrounds, which also is the site of GEODIS Park, home of the MLS Nashville SC soccer team. Put on some comfortable shoes, sharpen your negotiating skills, and expect to find practically anything under the sun.

401 Wingrove St., 615-862-5016
thefairgrounds.com/fleamarket

STOCK UP ON MUSIC
AT GRIMEY'S

There's probably a local ordinance that says you can't leave Nashville without buying some recorded music, and Grimey's New and Preloved Music and Books is a place you're guaranteed to find something you really, really want. In addition to vinyl and CDs, Grimey's has loads of books, T-shirts, postcards, and other merchandise. More importantly, Grimey's is a hot spot for artist appearances. The space is tiny, but you might chance into an in-store performance by someone such as Nikki Lane, Jessie Baylin, or Margo Price. Grimey's even is a venue for AMERICANAFEST (see page 34). It's a true Nashville experience to go record shopping and get a free live performance, too.

1060 E Trinity Ln., 615-226-3811
grimeys.com

TIP

There's a 10 percent discount on everything pre-loved on Tuesdays.

INHALE THE DELICIOUSNESS
OF CHRISTIE COOKIES

Have you ever smelled the almost intoxicating aroma of fresh chocolate chip cookies at a DoubleTree hotel? That's the aroma of Christie Cookies, a Nashville original just like Goo Goo Clusters and the Grand Ole Opry. Sending a mail-order tin of Christie Cookies will make you a hero in the eyes of the recipient—even if you send a tin to yourself. Nashvillians grew up with chocolate chip, white chocolate macadamia nut, and oatmeal raisin Christie Cookies, but the menu now has items such as lemon blueberry, snickerdoodle, and rocky road, plus triple chocolate brownies. All the ingredients are fresh, and as the bakers say, "We don't use preservatives or any other ingredients you can't pronounce." Stock up at two Nashville locations—1205 3rd Avenue North in Germantown and 2606 12th Avenue South in the 12South neighborhood.

800-458-2447
christiecookies.com

PICK AND GRIN
AT GRUHN GUITARS

All guitars are not created equal, but at Gruhn Guitars, every guitar in the store is beautiful—as are the banjos, mandolins, basses, and even ukuleles. This is fretted instrument heaven. The business opened in 1970 with 22 instruments—making it one of the first stores devoted to vintage and used fretted instruments—and now showcases more than 1,100. The store, which can seem as much art museum as music business—is renowned for appraising and repairing instruments. If you are a serious player or collector, you can ask the Gruhn Guitar staff to be on the lookout for the instruments of your dreams.

2120 8th Ave. S, 615-256-2033
guitars.com

TIP

Closer to downtown at 625 8th Avenue South is The North American Guitar, where you will find another awesome array of instruments and reminders of two respected names in Nashville music, Carter Vintage Guitars and Cotten Music Center. For details: thenorthamericanguitar.com

SHOP, DINE, AND LEARN
AT BELLE MEADE HISTORIC SITE

What today is called the Belle Meade Historic Site has transcended its former tourism identity as an antebellum mansion and little more. Its centerpiece remains the Greek Revival house that crowns its 32 acres, but it now is a place for gift shopping, wine and bourbon tasting, strolls in the woods, meat-and-three lunches, and even Segway tours. One of Nashville's earliest families established Belle Meade, which developed an international reputation in Thoroughbred horseracing. One of its studs, Bonnie Scotland, represents two-thirds of all Kentucky Derby winners. In recent years, Belle Meade has broadened its perspective, and its "Journey to Jubilee" tour tells a deep story about the enslaved people who helped build the estate's wealth.

110 Leake Ave., 615-356-0501
visitbellemeade.com

GO HISPANIC
AT PLAZA MARIACHI

Plaza Mariachi is a glorious conglomeration of Hispanic shops, restaurants, entertainment venues, and service businesses that are a wonderful use for a giant building that once was a Kroger supermarket. Las Adelitas has dresses for weddings and quinceañeras, Dulcería Morelia offers Mexican candies, Native Southwest sells Latin American clothing, Joyería la Central sparkles with jewelry, and the list goes on. Dining opportunities abound—consider Tres Gauchos for beef, Las Delicias for breads and desserts, and Paletas Tocumbo for agua frescas, ice cream, and paletas. Latin music is a major attraction, and the dance floor in front of the main stage is the place to prove your investment in salsa lessons was worthwhile.

3955 Nolensville Pike, 615-373-9292
plazamariachi.com

ACTIVITIES
BY SEASON

SPRING

SUMMER

FALL

WINTER

SUGGESTED
ITINERARIES

ORDER UP!

ONLY IN NASHVILLE

RETAIL THERAPY

RIGHT DOWNTOWN

JUST GET OUTDOORS

• •

FAMILY FUN

LET HISTORY ENLIGHTEN YOU

DATE NIGHT

• •

INDEX

• •

• •